"Full of snapshots of black history, Bryan Loritts's offering has given a tremendous gift to Christians who long to learn and rejoice in God's big story of grace to people from every nation, tribe, and tongue. You'll encounter a wide range of historical figures, some who will encourage you, others who will challenge you. But the story of Jesus and his saving work runs through all of it. Read and be encouraged."

Matthew J. Hall, provost of Biola University

"This is what Bryan Loritts does best—unearthing stories we haven't heard to reveal lessons we didn't know we needed. With a sharp eye for the overlooked and an innate gift for storytelling, he brings these moments to life in ways that challenge, inspire, and stay with you long after you've finished reading. Bryan is not just a collector of stories; he's a craftsman, weaving them into meaningful insights that resonate deeply. *Grace to Overcome* is Bryan doing his best work."

Janetta Oni, author of *Toxic Church*

"Bryan Loritts invites you on a daily experience at the crossroads of the presence and power of God and the historic journey of people of color. Seldom is there such a spiritual synthesis of holy revelation and historic affirmation of the sovereign presence of God in the earthly journey of people of faith. In the tone and tenor of the sovereignty of God in the lives of the displaced and often despised heroes of Israel, Dr. Loritts has sensitively and intentionally woven the revelation of the hand of God and the history of his sons and daughters of ebony hue into a daily call to gather at the junction of the display of the love of God in the lives of those often labeled the least, the last, and the lost."

Kenneth C. Ulmer, senior adviser to the president at Biola University

"Bryan Loritts's writing is both endearing and in-depth, comprehensive and clear. His personal vulnerability, historical scholarship, and theological precision shimmer in each devotional. Every page of this work will draw the reader into the deeper story of history and the thread of God's boundless grace that runs through it. This book may help you to understand humanity more fully, but it will do something more, something better—it will invite you to see Jesus more clearly. And isn't that the point? In Bryan's writing and preaching, it always is."

Priscilla Shirer, Bible teacher and author

"*Grace to Overcome* is a must-read that should be in every household! Bryan Loritts does a magnificent job interweaving the story of black people throughout history with Scripture and further helps the reader develop an appreciation for black history and the deep roots of Christianity within the black community. Bryan writes in a way that engulfs the reader in story and history just as he's always done as a preacher. Bryan has been influencing the hearts of people since the beginning of his ministry, and this work only further provides the evidence of the gift he has been to many, including me!"

Derrick Puckett, senior pastor of Renewal Church of Chicago and president of The Chicago Partnership

"Depth, balance, clarity, and creativity are words that come to mind when thinking of this resource. This symphonic resource merges history, story, and the Bible for the mind and the heart all in one. My dear friend Bryan Loritts has graciously kept all of us from separating our sociality from our theology; he doesn't call us to put our sociology before our theology but the other way around. Seeing the redemptive story of God in any history is amazing; however, seeing this metanarrative in black history is a gift for all of us to continue to see it in our lives today."

Eric Mason, founder and lead pastor of Epiphany Fellowship

"I read these devotionals and remember who I am, who we are, and who God is. *Grace to Overcome* connects us to God's grace throughout history and proves our miracle is not over or waiting to unfold. It is now."

Renée Elise Goldsberry, Tony Award– and Grammy Award–winning artist

"Speaking to the heart of our present moment, Bryan Loritts presents a powerfully composed amalgamation of hope and heritage that illuminates the faith, tenacity, and collective contributions of the black diaspora. Encouraged through the lens of Scripture, we are called to remember, to reckon, and to rise. Loritts lifts history from the pages of time and sets it before us as a beautiful living testament to God's sovereign hand at work. This book doesn't merely inform—it provokes, it stirs the soul, and it calls us to action. With these masterfully articulated devotions, Dr. Loritts has done it again."

Ricky Jenkins, senior pastor of Southwest Church in Indian Wells, California

BRYAN C. LORITTS

Foreword by CHARLIE DATES

GRACE TO OVERCOME

31 Devotions on God's Work Through Black History

An imprint of InterVarsity Press
Downers Grove, Illinois

InterVarsity Press
P.O. Box 1400 | Downers Grove, IL 60515-1426
ivpress.com | email@ivpress.com

InterVarsity Press® is the publishing division of InterVarsity Christian Fellowship/USA®. For more information, visit intervarsity.org.

Published in association with the literary agency of Wolgemuth & Wilson.

Cover design: Faceout Studio, Molly von Borstel
Interior design: Daniel van Loon
Images: © EZEEproject / DigitalVision Vectors via Getty Images

ISBN 978-1-5140-1191-1 (print) | ISBN 978-1-5140-1193-5 (digital)

Printed in the United States of America ♾

Library of Congress Cataloging-in-Publication Data
A catalog record for this book is available from the Library of Congress.

32 31 30 29 28 27 26 25 | 12 11 10 9 8 7 6 5 4 3 2 1

TO

CRAWFORD WHEELER LORITTS SR. (1914–1995)

AND

SYLVIA GRAY LORITTS (1922–1997)

My Pop-Pop and Nana, who endured Jim Crow with pride and dignity, and received much grace to overcome.

CONTENTS

FOREWORD

CHARLIE DATES

His name is Orenthal James Simpson. You know him as "The Juice.'"

These were the opening words to the first sermon I ever heard Bryan Loritts preach. I was a senior at the University of Illinois attending an IMPACT Conference over winter break. His sermon that day was titled "Standing in Babylon." In an exposition from the book of Daniel, Loritts aimed to help us discern how to live for God in an idol-rich culture hell-bent against the ethics of the gospel. He wanted us to stand in Babylon. That was some twenty years ago, but if you were to press me right now, I could preach more than half of that sermon from memory.

I remember it so well because Bryan is a stellar storyteller. Almost effortlessly, he turned our ears into eyes. The other, more meaningful reason I remember it is that the story he told that day had meaning attached.

So many stories are told today . . . with so little meaning attached to them. You can find them a dime a dozen in political stump speeches and sermons alike. What a tragedy it is to listen to a speaker and feel no real application—to listen to a message with no real transformative impact from the narratives they tell. I sometimes feel that way when listening to some of our popular comedians. Their stories are engaging and hilarious, but unlike Richard Pryor or Dave Chappelle, their comedic narratives carry no further significance. They leave us with no lasting impulse for change.

We need more stories with meaning, more timely anecdotes that help us interpret life. We need a fresh telling of relevant incidents that carry significance for today. What's more: our world is better when these narratives are true and historical.

If you feel my particular burden, we need these historical narratives from the experience of African American Christ-followers. After all, we have come over a way that with tears has been watered, treading our path through the blood of the slaughtered. The intersection of faith with the unique African American story is perhaps the most timely message for America today. It's not just a story that we read, but a story that reads us.

This is the kind of book you will want to offer to your children in years to come. Do that. Bequeath this to the next generation—not because history will repeat itself, but because the future has a way of harmonizing with the past. And I think that's how faith grows.

INTRODUCTION

CUL-DE-SACS

Some years ago, my family—that's my wife, Korie, our boys, and me—packed up our things and headed out to Arizona to spend Thanksgiving with Korie's relatives. A few days in, my wife thought it would be great to take us on a tour of her old stomping grounds. When we told our sons what we would be up to for the next several hours, the look on their faces said, "Anything but this."

Off we went. We pulled into the apartment complex where Korie spent her preschool years. She pointed to a patch of grass in the middle of the buildings which once had swing sets and seesaws. As she shared her memories, I could almost see Korie holding court among her girlfriends on the playground. We could hear the laughter as she told stories about her adventures on the swing set. And I could see her mother standing on the balcony of their apartment, telling Korie it was time to come in for dinner.

Next was the Catholic church her family attended on major holidays. A few miles down the road was the home they eventually settled into, but not for long. Korie didn't look at the front yard of the home at the end of the cul-de-sac the way she looked at the playground in the apartment complex. This grassy area was filled with painful memories, like the day her family split apart, sending Korie and her mom one way and her dad and sister another. It felt like we were at a funeral.

Then there was the all-girls Catholic high school Korie attended. We tried to pull into the parking lot, but the gate was closed, so we could only peer at the complex through the fence. Korie talked about the place as if she was telling a story about someone else's life—distant, detached. My wife is half Mexican and half Irish, and this was the school where the wealthy people from Scottsdale (or "Snottsdale," as some call it) sent their kids. Korie did not come from money; she was only able to attend because she earned a need-based scholarship. Once enrolled, Korie learned the school's harsh social dynamics: her Mexican features excluded her from some people, but the fact she was raised by her Irish mother meant she did not speak Spanish, which put her on the outs with other Latinas. After a few moments of silence, we piled back in the car. Korie wanted to make one more stop.

By this time, we were all starving and more than pleased when my wife guided the car into a little Mexican joint that must have been built somewhere around the year we were sending soldiers off to fight in Vietnam. The sign reminded me of those old Las Vegas hotel and casino signs, announcing to all who drove by that Frank Sinatra and the Rat Pack would be in concert that evening. The whole vibe of the place had me rubbing my hands together in excitement over what I just knew would be some of the best, most authentic Mexican food I had ever eaten.

Wrong. The food was awful, like, really, *really* bad. You know the food is bad when your young adult sons, who do not discriminate when it comes to food, say it's bad. Korie smiled and agreed. But then she told us that this was the spot her family would visit every Friday night for dinner. This was before the big breakup on the lawn of the house at the end of the cul-de-sac. This was when times were good, and all was right in her home.

What she was really eating wasn't the bad tortilla, but the laughter of family together for their weekly ritual. This was before the big late-night arguments, before she started finding either of her parents passed out from another episode of drinking. She wanted to end the day on a good note, conjuring up great memories. For us, the place was just bad food; to Korie, it was great memories.

"Can we please go home now?" one of our kids begged. Honestly, I kind of got where he was coming from. We had spent the last six hours crammed in a little rental car visiting places we had never seen before, which seemed to have had no bearing on our lives. And if I can keep it a buck with you: this was November in Arizona. The weather was amazing, and I love golf. Do you know how many courses we passed during our jaunt down memory lane? It did cross my mind more than a few times to just hurry Korie along so I could get nine holes in. But I didn't.

The Mexican food spot was our last stop, thankfully, but I felt as if I needed to say something to my exasperated son. I affirmed his feelings, agreeing that we had spent a lot of time visiting places and hearing stories that seemed to have nothing to do with us. But I told him that since Mom is family, her history is our history. I pointed out that the highs and lows of her experiences as a biracial woman in high school shaped her into the compassionate yet fierce mother of triracial children today, who would advocate on their behalf and stand up to anyone she remotely felt had slighted them. "Where did that come from?" I asked. "It came right from her experiences at the all-girls high school."

He also needed to know how his mother used to work for a prominent news station, but chose to quit when she became pregnant with him so that she could attend every event in his life. She never wanted him to know the pain of looking around and seeing everyone's parents show up for the school spelling bee except for his—a pain she was well acquainted with once her parents went their separate ways.

Oh, and while I was at it (I was on a roll now), I felt he should know the reason his mom and I were still married, even though we had been through very tough times. Why? Because of her fierce determination to never let her children experience the ever-present ache of divorce, the ache which seeped into her nine-year-old heart as she waved a tearful goodbye to her dad and sister.

I wish I could tell you that our boys instantly went from exasperation to jubilation over what I shared, but that's not what happened. At most they grunted, "Oh, okay," put their earbuds in, and listened to some music. Still, I'd like to believe those six hours of history connected our kids more to their mom. I know they did for me.

COLORBLINDNESS AND THE QUESTION OF BLACK HISTORY

I'd also like to believe there will come a day when my sons will find themselves in the passenger seat of a rental car as their wife takes them around her old stomping grounds, conjuring up pleasant and tear-filled memories of her past. Hopefully, they will be more empathetic. I hope they will come to see the vital role history plays in human connection.

We each come with a story, and there is no way we can have a substantive relationship with one another unless we see the essential pieces of each other's narrative. It's important we unearth the story of black history and the possibility it holds for weighty intimacy across the divide. There are many who wonder, *Why do we even need to talk about black history?* You've probably heard some of our white siblings question why we even need a black history month. They might follow up by asking why we don't have a white history month. Isn't the very name and endeavor of "black history" divisive?

And to be fair, it's not just our white siblings who have questioned the whole project of black history; so have many members of minority groups. In her novel *Americanah,* Nigerian writer Chimamanda Ngozi Adichie has her African protagonist go on about how she didn't know she was black until she came to America. Here, Adichie gently reminds the reader that not all black people see themselves naturally as black. Morgan Freeman would agree. In a 2005 interview with Mike Wallace, Freeman said that the best way to combat racism is to not mention race at all, to just sidestep any notion of our embodied differences.[1] As you can imagine, his remarks caused a firestorm, especially given his identity as a black man.

Many would find Freeman's colorblind ideology a welcome path for moving beyond racism. But there are several problems with Freeman's suggestion. Some would argue there is only one race of people—the human race—and while that may be true biologically, race in America has primarily focused on a social construct, a system where people are valued or devalued based on the color of their skin. Freeman's reaction, like so many others, conflates biology with the social construct.

The Bible offers us a different path, where our individual ethnicities are actually a part of what it means to be made in the image of God. The Christian worldview maintains that ethnicity is not something we will just be forced to deal with on earth, but will be a part of our eternal redemptive future (Revelation 5:9-10). And since this is the biblical worldview, I shouldn't view my ethnicity either as a result of somebody's sin, or as either good or bad luck. It's a part of God's good design for me. When the Bible says we are fearfully and wonderfully made, excuse my language, but that ain't just our spirits, y'all (Psalm 139:14). It's also our bodies, our ethnicities.

As embodied people made in the image of God, our ethnicity is part of God's intended will. We would be wrong to ignore ethnicity.

I really do get why people would choose not to talk about race or ethnicity. If you want to put yourself on a collision course with an awkward moment, just bring up the subject. But it's impossible to have an enduring, substantive relationship with anyone while ignoring whole dimensions of their lives. Korie used to chide me about my "perfect" family. My parents have been married for well over fifty years, and genuinely love and enjoy each other. This is not Korie's story. So when she talks about the pain of her parents' divorce and how it continues to impact her, I cannot really relate. In the early years of marriage, when I was more like my unempathetic "Can't we just go home now?" son, I wanted to tell my wife that her story had nothing to do with me. Why couldn't we just move on? While I never said those words, my heart posture was one big eye roll. What God wants in my marriage is oneness, a soul-level harmony with my wife, and we have no shot at getting there unless we do things like eating at bad restaurants and stopping at old playgrounds, Catholic high schools, and cul-de-sacs. History really does matter in our journey into unity.

Lately, there's been a movement to remove black history in several states. In December 2023, a Missouri school board voted to drop elective courses in black history and literature.[2] In February 2023, the *New York Times* reported on Florida's efforts to significantly pare down major sections of black history taught in schools.[3] Some would push back by defending Florida's governor, saying he's only getting rid of the liberal parts of black history (like critical race theory or queer theory). Now, I am a Christ-follower whose worldview is primarily shaped by the authority of the Scriptures—not just my lived experience. But while there are plenty of historical ideologies that I disagree with, since when did history register to vote, aligning itself with a political party? Of course, history *contains* liberals and conservatives, Democrats and Republicans, but in the main, the events of history do not fit into any of these ideologies. To remove sections of history we deem to be in conflict with our beliefs is akin to removing a chapter of a book, rendering the whole thing impossible to make sense of or even read.

These wonderful people in states like Missouri and Florida would do well to remember that the question of history centers more around *why* than *should*. Though critically informative, history's first impulse is not with telling us what we should do in the present, but if listened to carefully, whispers as to how and why we got here. For example, did you know we can pinpoint the exact moment when black people broadly swung Democrat? It was a phone call from John F. Kennedy to a frightened Coretta Scott King in the fall of 1960, when Coretta was frantic over what would become of her incarcerated husband, Martin (more on that later). Because of that one call, the black press, along with Dr. King's father and a host of black pastors, put out a nationwide campaign to get blacks to vote Democrat. It worked. Kennedy, the Democratic presidential candidate, won, and blacks in the main have voted Democrat ever since. Think about that—one ninety-second empathy-filled call changed a whole group of people.

The lesson from this historic moment is not whether black people *should* vote Democrat. Instead, the lesson centers around *why* black people continued to vote Democrat in such large numbers. History says it all comes down to one word—*empathy*. While the Republican nominee Nixon showed none, Kennedy took an opposite route, signaling his deep care and concern.

I write these words well over sixty years removed from Kennedy's well-timed, empathetic phone call to an anxious Coretta King, yet history's lesson is still informative, holding forth profound hope if we would just lean in together and listen. The last few election cycles have proven to be historically combative and divisive. Like a car stuck in the mud, human relations across color, class, and ideological lines have left our tires spinning because we have stalled on the question of *should*, instead of doing the deeper work of getting to history's lesson of *why*. What has been missing from our very heated exchanges over whether one should vote for people with an established reputation for endorsing the mass slaughter of babies in utero, is the human necessity of empathy. Did Kennedy's politics align with King's? Given the brevity of Kennedy's life, history shrugs its shoulders. Nonetheless, Kennedy picked up the phone and placed a call to a family. In his own way, he communicated, "We may see this differently, but I am with you."

In the early days of our marriage, Korie and I had a running conflict that I was convinced would never end. I've never been much of a drinker, but when I would order the occasional glass of wine, she would shut down and mutter something under her breath like, "I wish you wouldn't do that." Immediately an argument would ensue, and what was supposed to be a fun date night would turn into conflict and an early return home. I just could not understand what the big deal was. If the government said I could drink, surely my wife should get on board.

Everything changed when I went beyond what I thought Korie *should* do to *why* she was so bothered by my glass of wine. In vulnerability she took me back to the cul-de-sacs of her life, sharing with me that everyone she loved had abused alcohol. Getting to the *why* of her history sparked empathy in my heart and led us to deeper levels of intimacy and unity.

Why is it important we learn about the gang rape of Recy Taylor, the murder of Emmett Till, or the Forsyth race riots of 1912? These tragic events, along with a host of others, have evoked a suspicious, questioning posture among so many blacks today who embody the trauma of our ancestors. Should we be more trusting? Should blacks hold to an innocent-until-proven-guilty disposition when it comes to whites? Should blacks be so quick to get angry or jump to conclusions? These questions may be fair, but they do not go far enough. Let us not be so quick to stop at *should*, but press deeper into *why*. In that answer lies a far greater answer for the lingering divide of our present moment—empathy.

THE PROBLEM OF ETHNIC IDOLATRY

A colorblind posture to the subject of race is not the only problem we have before us in our quest for unity. At the other extreme is what I call ethnic idolatry, where we find our ultimate meaning in our embodied selves. Of course, one of my aims in writing *Grace to Overcome* is to provide a sense of dignity to African Americans. If you are in this category, I hope that as you read stories of great inventors, adventurers, and heroes among our people, you come away feeling a few inches taller. But if dignity is all you feel, then I have not served you well.

Ethnic idolatry not only fails to move the needle when we talk about ethnic unity, it actually works against it. While my story as a black man made in the image of God is a part of his good design and intentions for me, it will only reach fullness when I connect it to the much larger story of what God is doing in the souls of humanity throughout time.

The sojourn of black folks in America has been arduous, but along the way we have brought about some of the most profound sociological change any society in world history has ever seen. Even an amateur historian can readily see how this came about: African Americans have always drawn a straight line between our experience in the foreign, hostile land of the United States to that of Israel, the covenant people of God in Egypt. Our ancestors viewed their narrative not as an end unto itself, but as a subplot within the grander story of what God was doing in the world. We understood that our strength to overcome was really a *grace* to overcome because we hitched our lived experience as exiles to the broader, more powerful narrative of the God who gave us what we needed to endure.

In writing on the effectiveness of Frederick Douglass, the most photographed man of the nineteenth century, biographer David Blight points to "the guiding theme" of Douglass, who grounded all of his speaking, writing, and justice efforts "in the Bible, especially the Old Testament."[4] It's more than possible that Douglass's framework of seeing the narrative of the black experience as a part of a much broader, biblical one was influenced by the likes of Sojourner Truth. Truth was not only an advocate for racial and gender justice, but also a preacher who saw herself and her people as moral kin to the suffering Israelites. The arc of her advocacy was not ultimately located in her blackness or her gender, but in her faith.

And who could ever forget the rainy night in Memphis, Tennessee, when Dr. Martin Luther King Jr. would make his way one last time to the pulpit, where he likened himself to the prophet Moses and his ethnic kin to the people of Israel. It was an act of love that cast him off his sickbed there at the Lorraine Motel, where he would make his way into the Mason Temple. On this rainy night, he gathered all the hope he could and poured it out onto his weary audience, pointing out that just as Israel had made it to the promised land, they, too, as black people would make it to the promised land. What's more, King saw himself as Moses, the one who led the people through the wilderness but would not go with them into the land flowing with milk and honey. Drawing on this narrative, King wondered whether he would get to the other side of the Jordan with his people. Alas, he would not. I'd like to believe that what thrust him out of bed those few hours before his death was not the experience of black people in America, but the story of Israel, the biblical people of God.

Time does not permit me to flood you with more examples of blacks who saw themselves as part of the biblical story, extracting the sustenance and strength they needed in each moment to endure and flourish in their own crucible of suffering. This is not to say every influential black person in American history has been a Christian, or even remotely religious. For every Frederick Douglass, Sojourner Truth, and Martin Luther King, there is a Langston Hughes, Nikki Giovanni, or Richard Pryor. And yet, when we zoom out on black history, we see the dominant, hope-filled role the church and a deep, abiding faith played in sustaining us during the midnight hour of slavery and Jim Crow.

In the following pages you will encounter their stories and see how I have sought to link biblical passages to a lesson or theme of their experience. Though a black history devotional might seem like a novelty, the notion of connecting a biblical passage to a black historical figure is anything but; it's how we've always lived. In fact, this project connecting the embodied experience of black people with the metanarrative of Scripture is not a ploy to sell books or an innovative idea for how to nourish your own soul, but an exercise in history. It is the same historical tradition in which every Sunday black folks would put on their finest clothes, sit on wooden pews, and listen as the preacher would make a beeline from Israel's history and the cross of Jesus Christ to the streets of Selma, Chicago, Harlem, or whatever neighborhood where they had congregated.

Times indeed have changed. With the legislative advances of the 1960s, the doors of economic opportunity for African Americans have slowly opened, and so have another set of doors—the exit doors to the black church. Recent data reveals an astonishing exodus of blacks from the faith.[5] For the first time in American history, African Americans are decoupling their ethnicity from the broader story of the Bible in unprecedented numbers. There are many reasons for this: the perception of Christianity being a white man's religion, displacement from historic black communities in urban centers and black churches, or the easing of communal suffering in a post–Jim Crow world and the way it used to gather and galvanize us (this is not to say that we live in a post-racial society).

But I am concerned that the black community is missing the nucleus of our collective history, which has always been anchored in the story of the Bible. This is why in the pages to come, I not only offer historical moments, but tether those scenes to the story of Scripture. If you are black, you may not be a Christian or even believe in the Bible—but chances are, your Big Mama or Madea did.

If you are not African American, your curiosity should be piqued by the question of what made blacks so historically resilient. How in the world did we make it in the face of such suffering and oppression? Maybe as you see the ties between the arc of Scripture and the arc of the black experience, you might come away inspired to anchor your experience to something outside of yourself.

Finally, I'd love to offer two suggestions to guide us in our tour through black history. The first is to digest *Grace to Overcome* in community with others. People who are not African American need to hear from those who are as it relates to these pivotal moments in American history. But black people also need to hear from those of other ethnicities how they are processing what may be new information. Both communities need to lean in and do the work of not only stitching these moments to the larger project of American history, but also gleaning spiritual strength to consider Christianity or deepen one's walk with Christ. Ask questions like, "How did today's reading make you feel?" I am hopeful these snippets will spark dialogue across the ethnic divide to move us closer toward one another.

The last thing to be considered is that given the devotional nature of the book, these black history moments are just that—moments. There is no way to cover each person or event completely. People are nuanced and complex, but for the sake of time those complexities will mostly be absent from this devotional. I appreciate your graciousness toward me as you interact with the pages to come.

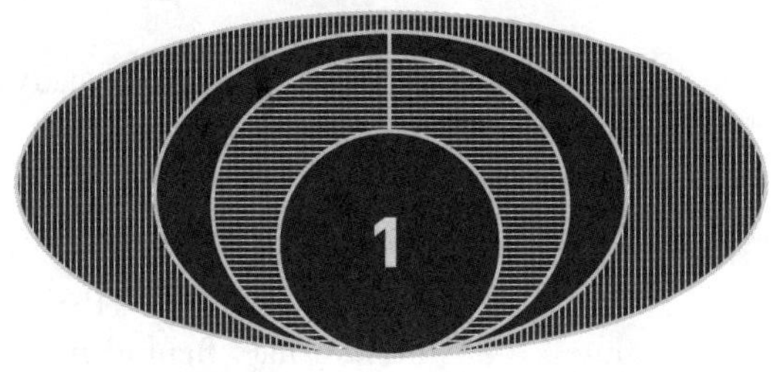

JESSE NEEDS A HUG

"This is my beloved Son, with whom I am well pleased."

MATTHEW 3:17

The 1936 Olympic Games in Berlin, Germany were supposed to showcase what Adolf Hitler deemed to be the superiority of the Aryan race. Jesse Owens (1913–1980), however, would frustrate those intentions; he would go on to win a record four gold medals. One of those medals was in an event Owens came dangerously close to not qualifying for—the long jump. Having missed on his first two opportunities to qualify, the pressure on Owens was obvious as he knelt in prayer for his final attempt.

As Jesse described it, it was at this moment that his German opponent, Carl Ludwig "Luz" Long (1913–1943), walked over and hugged him, while Hitler and the world watched. Jesse said that he drew calm and encouragement from Carl, that he went on to not only win the event but gain a friend. Later, after the finals round took place, the black Jesse Owens stood with his gold medal draped around his neck, while he saluted the American flag. Behind him was Carl, donning his silver medal, giving the Nazi salute. All under the gaze of the Nazi regime.

The date was August 3, 1936.

In the years to come, their paths would go in different directions. Jesse came back to America as a celebrated hero who had to face the indignities of Jim Crow. He struggled to make ends meet, even running against horses and cars to earn income. Carl would find himself in the German army in the middle of World War II, stationed in North Africa. Yet through it all Jesse said they remained the closest of friends.

In his last letter to Jesse, Carl wrote,

> My heart tells me, if I be honest with you, that this is the last letter I shall ever write. If it is so, I ask you something. It is a something so very important to me. It is you go to Germany when this war done, someday find my Karl [Kai], and tell him about his father. Tell him, Jesse, what times were like when we not separated by war. I am saying—tell him how things can be between men on this earth.[1]

Not long after these words, Carl was killed in the battle of St. Pietro, on the Italian island of Sardinia, on July 14, 1943, just shy of seven years since meeting Owens.

The first time I read this story I was moved to the brink of tears. I was also filled with hope to continue the work of bridge building across the racial divide. If God could bring together a black American and a white German who would later become a part of the Nazi regime, then surely there's hope for us. I remember reading this story and thinking, "And there's not a movie about this friendship because . . . ?"

Because it's not true.

Come to find out, Jesse Owens made just about all of it up. Of the thousands of people who were at the stadium that day, not one remembered seeing a black Jesse Owens hugging a white German. Not even reporters on the field, like the famed American Grantland Rice, could recall the moment. And then there's Jesse Owens's own confession late in life of how he had constructed this lie.[2] So why did Jesse tell this story over and over and over again?

No one can really pinpoint the exact moment when Jesse began this fiction. But it seems to have become a part of the Jesse Owens legend in the early 1950s, when he went back to Germany to speak to audiences. By then a lot had transpired in Jesse's life, most of which was tragic. This champion was still struggling to eke out an existence and find acceptance in his own nation steeped in institutionalized racism.

How would you feel if despite your world-record-breaking performances, you were still barred from sleeping in certain hotels, couldn't earn any mainstream endorsement deals, and you were forced to race animals and cars just to put food on the table, all because you were black? And how would you feel when just weeks after the 1936 Olympic Games, you were banned for life by the widely-regarded-as-racist Avery Brundage, president of the US Olympic Committee?

The way I see it, Jesse was slowly coming to terms with the fact that no amount of performance could truly give him the acceptance he wanted. None of his gold medals could give him a sense of belonging. So some years after the Games, he began to tell this tall tale of a German man helping him out at the Olympics. He probably didn't mean it as some tear-jerker story but more as a fable: "See, if the worst of the worst would accept me, then maybe people from my own country would too."

And what I think Jesse was after is what all of us are after. We all want to be valued for who we are, not our performance—no matter how great that performance may be. We long to be cherished not because of our looks, money, status, or pedigree, but just for our intrinsic worth as human beings.

When Jesus emerges from the baptism waters in the third chapter of Matthew, we hear God say these words of him: "This is my beloved Son, with whom I am well pleased" (Matthew 3:17). Keep in mind, God gives these words of acceptance and affirmation *before* Jesus performed a miracle, picked a disciple, or preached a sermon. With these words God embraces his Son and says, "You are accepted. Period. End of story."

If you are in Christ, you need to know that what God said of Jesus, he says of you and me. We are his sons and daughters, with whom he is well pleased. God can say this with integrity not because we earned his hug, but because when we surrendered to Christ, the righteousness of his son Jesus was transferred to our lives (Romans 5). Before we performed that act of generosity, or led someone to Christ, or made the right choice, God hugged us, saying we are accepted in him. We don't need to tell any tall tales in search of someone's embrace or approval. No need to set any world records of good deeds in the hopes that someone will invite us into their group, because we are already in the group that really matters—the family of God. We are loved as is.

And if you do not call yourself a Christian, you can, right now, experience the embrace of Father God, who loves you so much he sent his only son to die for you.

Receiving God's hug is ground zero of the Christian life. Everything we do flows from a posture of either acceptance by God or attempts to perform. I can tell you that going down the performance road is an exercise in exhaustion. I have a friend who begins every day by extending her arms outward, imagining herself feeling the embrace of God. She whispers to God that she will live out of a posture of acceptance and love. This frees her, she says, from not only the applause of others, but to really love people well. I like that, and so should you. You may want to make my friend's daily habit your own. Go ahead, drink it in: God says to you, "You are my beloved, with whom I am well pleased."

MILES'S BACK

Do not think that I have come to bring peace to the earth. I have not come to bring peace, but a sword. For I have come to set a man against his father, and a daughter against her mother, and a daughter-in-law against her mother-in-law. And a person's enemies will be those of his own household. Whoever loves father or mother more than me is not worthy of me, and whoever loves son or daughter more than me is not worthy of me. And whoever does not take his cross and follow me is not worthy of me. Whoever finds his life will lose it, and whoever loses his life for my sake will find it.

MATTHEW 10:34-39

Artists in a capitalist society live in the tension between the freedom of expression and the necessity to eat. There is the pull to be "me," but what happens when being "me" doesn't sell enough to pay the rent? When the art overpowers the business, we get the phrase "starving artists." And when the business becomes greater than the artist, we get expressions like "sellout." Every artist feels this twoness, this push and pull. And the situation was even more extreme for black artists back in the era of Jim Crow.

Take Louis Armstrong (1901–1971), who for much of his career played with the business in mind. Armstrong was determined to not rock the boat. He'd play nice, flash his teeth and slap his leg, and howl with his trademark gravelly voice in order to ingratiate himself to his audience, all in the hopes they would buy his records and extend more invitations. His antics grated on the younger generation of blacks, and especially Miles Davis (1926–1991).

Miles was the antithesis of Louis. One rarely saw his teeth, because Miles was not known to smile. Promoters found him to be a pain in their backside. Musicians were regularly the object of his outbursts. And while Miles played to mostly white crowds, it was common to see this world-famous trumpeter play with his back to them, sending the abrasive message that he was no Louis Armstrong. While you saw Armstrong's teeth, you were likely to get Davis's back. Davis was so bent on being respected as a black man that he used disrespect as a sort of currency to get what he wanted.

With all of this, you would think Miles's career would be short-lived. Not even close. His music was so good, people were willing to look past his behavior to hear his trumpet. Miles would be nominated for over thirty Grammys and win eight of them. He would also be the lead musician in what would become the bestselling jazz album of all time—*Kind of Blue*.

There's something to be said of a man who is so secure, so free in what he has and who he is, he's not afraid to offend paying customers.

And I think that's the allure of Jesus. Our Savior was no Louis Armstrong—flashing a smile while he sequestered his real thoughts, all in an effort to gain a large following. In fact, there were many times when Jesus was more than comfortable with offending people, playing with his proverbial back to the audience. In a very direct moment, Jesus said explicitly that he had come to bring division among families (Matthew 10:34-37). In a Middle Eastern culture like the one Jesus was talking to, family was everything. Family was what brought you security and status. You trained in the family business to one day take it over. You married with the expectation of having kids who could continue the family legacy. And you held onto and took care of the family land that had been passed to you because familial property secured your place in society.

To the Jews of Jesus' day, family wasn't just important—family was everything. For Jesus to say he had come to disrupt the family structure would have been about the most offensive thing a person could say. No, Jesus doesn't hate families. Instead, his hope is that people should so prioritize him that if they had to, they would be willing to leave their own families for Jesus.

In a weird way, what makes Jesus God is the ease in which he is okay with offending us. A God who never unsettles me, who never at times plays with his back to me, is no God. A God who always agrees with me and makes me comfortable is no God. If I believe this, God just looks like *me*; I'm crafting a deity after my image, likeness, and likings. We need a God who is free enough and loves us enough that he challenges us out of the status quo, even risking our loyalty to him.

When Miles played with his back to the Jim Crow audiences of the mid-twentieth century, he was shaking the very structures of his society. And when Jesus spoke in Matthew 10, he was rattling the very things Jews held onto for life. Today, this same Jesus is willing to play with his back to me at times, calling out the idols of my heart so that I can experience the freedom he has come to bring. The question is, what will you do when Jesus inevitably offends you? How do you respond when he calls you to give up that possession or person? How do you handle it when it's clear he's asking you to apologize, or let go of that thing which has become an idol in your life? Will you get up from the table and leave, or will you bend to his invitation?

And when it comes to your relationships with others, how often do you play with your back to them? (I'm not talking about rejecting people, but holding a willingness to have healthy conflict.) Are you more Louis Armstrong or Miles Davis? Do you just smile all the time to others, not wanting to have hard conversations because you want to be accepted and liked by them? Or will you at times have the courage to be like Miles? To love someone is to do whatever it takes to bring out the best in them. At times this means the willingness to offend—not because you are contentious or rude, but because you love them too much to let them continue in a destructive habit. To be a good friend, to really love our neighbor as the Bible commands, means that at times they will have to see our backs.

My middle son is the most creative person I know. He couldn't care less about what you think. He wears leather jackets in the summer, has tattoos all over the place, and sports more piercings than I have bothered to count. He's also a deep lover of Jesus, outspoken about his faith, and loves to read philosophy and challenge people with his contrarian thinking. I find myself envious of his freedom. And while there are a few qualities I'm praying he doesn't emulate about the jazz musician, I am grateful to have named him Myles.

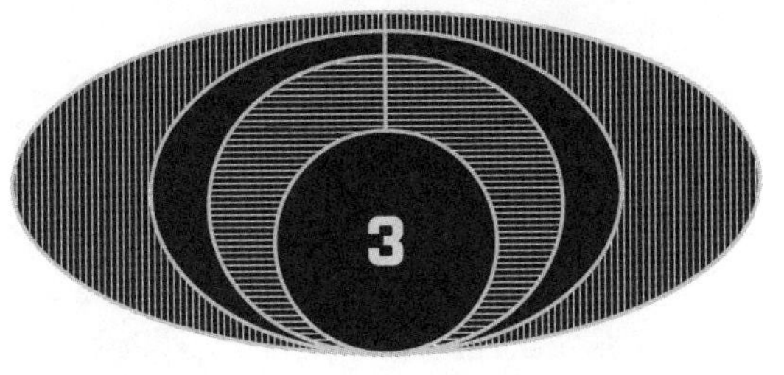

THANK GOD FOR A PRAYING MAMA

She was deeply distressed and prayed to the LORD and wept bitterly. And she vowed a vow and said, "O LORD of hosts, if you will indeed look on the affliction of your servant and remember me and not forget your servant, but will give to your servant a son, then I will give him to the LORD all the days of his life, and no razor shall touch his head."

1 SAMUEL 1:10-11

As a young girl, she suffered from polio and scarlet fever. Her initial prognosis was bleak; she was told she would never walk again. Born in the deep South at the height of Jim Crow, no hospitals within fifty miles would treat her because of the color of her skin. Her mother, Blanche, who was employed as a domestic for a white family, finagled her schedule so she could drive her daughter over fifty miles one way to the only hospital that would see her. Blanche did this twice a week for years, all while fighting tears as she watched her child hop around on one leg.

And then there was progress . . .

At eight she could move around with a leg brace. At eleven, much to her horror and delight, Blanche caught her playing basketball. Eventually her daughter would turn to sports and become an All-American basketball player. But it was on the track where she shone; she took home the bronze for the 4x400 relay in the 1956 Olympic Games. Then, in 1960, she broke several world records on her way to three gold medals.

On her return home from the 1960 Olympics, she got word that her hometown, which had once refused to treat her for polio because she was black, wanted to throw her a parade. Wilma Rudolph (1940–1994) said she would—but only on the condition the parade was integrated. They agreed.

I wonder what was going through Wilma's mind as she sat in the backseat of the car, inching her way down the road as people lined up on either side to catch a glimpse of her. Surely, she had never seen such a strange, mixed gathering. But her mother, who was sitting next to her in that car, must have enjoyed the irony as well; a different kind of irony. All of these people had come out to see the Olympic gold medal winner and world record breaker who, just a few years before, was hopping around on one foot.

While the town was right to honor Wilma Rudolph, we would do well to give her mother Blanche her flowers too. Looking back over her life, Wilma reflected, "My doctor told me I would never walk again. My mother told me I would. I believed my mother."[1] What turned a polio-stricken child into the fastest woman in the world? A mama who refused to take no for an answer . . . even from a so-called expert.

In the black church, Mother's Day is a significant moment on the calendar when we rearrange our services to honor the mothers in our midst. Many times, the pastor will use this occasion to take a break from whatever series they have been preaching to deliver a word of hope and encouragement to the backbone of the black community. They draw on the stories of mothers like Hannah in 1 Samuel, who model an extraordinary Blanche-like faith.

When we first meet Hannah, she is walking the path of infertility. It's more than easy to imagine her emotions, especially when we consider the times in which she lives. Her culture sees a woman's value as being connected to her ability to have children. Yet as gutted as Hannah may feel, she never loses hope. Like Blanche with her feeble child, Hannah will not give up. She prays to God, asking him to not only give her a child, but a son. God hears that prayer and gives her a son, and Hannah makes good on her promise by dedicating him back to God.

Her son's name is Samuel, and he goes on to be a man who loves God and leads the nation of Israel with integrity. Score another one for a faith-filled, praying mother.

And what about you? What are the so-called "experts" telling you can never happen? What walls have you faced? Maybe, like Hannah, you're dealing with infertility, or, like Blanche, caring for a feeble child. Or maybe it's other "impossibilities" like finances. Or maybe you're desperate to find work. Whatever it may be, don't stop believing. Remember who is on the other end of your prayers. That's right—the same God who blessed Hannah with a son and strengthened Wilma's legs is more than able to answer your prayers.

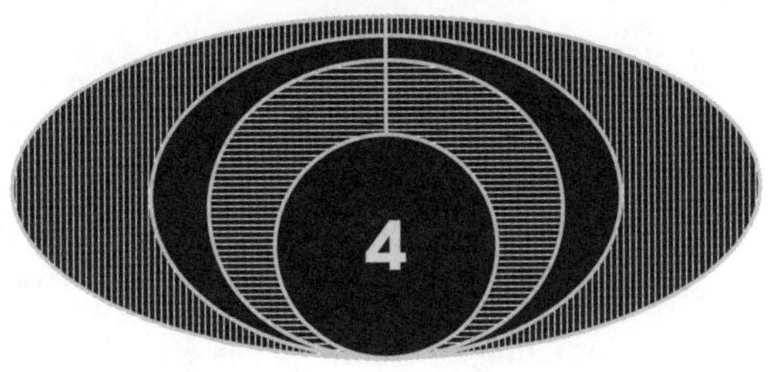

THE GODFATHER OF DIGNITY

For we are his workmanship.

Ephesians 2:10

2020 was a year we will not soon forget. The tragic murder of George Floyd, and the worldwide outcry it sparked. A global pandemic. A contentious presidential election. And the pervasive feeling that our democracy was on the brink.

As bad as things were in 2020, if you were over sixty years old you may have had a sense of déjà vu—an ominous feeling you had seen this before.

If 2020 is looking for its father, 1968 might as well take a paternity test. The two look very much alike. The killing of a black man (Martin Luther King Jr.) followed by riots across our nation. A hotly contested presidential race. A deeply divided country. With the black community left without its leader, what were we to do? The answer came from the "Godfather of Soul," James Brown (1933–2006). Having cut his trademark perm, along with a new record, James emerged with the black empowerment anthem *Say It Loud, I'm Black and I'm Proud* (1968).

The record is quintessential Brown, as he begins the song with his familiar grunt ("UH!"). And then, drawing on the colloquialism of his time, he says to his black listeners, "With your bad self!" And when Brown finally says over and over again to "say it loud, I'm black and I'm proud," that chorus is akin to a coach lifting the heads of his wearied team at the end of a hard-fought contest that they lost.

What you may not know about the godfather's anthem is that the voices on the chorus beckoning people to "say it loud" were white and Asian children. This was an intentional move by Brown, because while he understood dignity came from within, he also knew the power of other people outside of our community affirming the message of self-worth. Dignity, as James understood it, was best played as a team sport.

Paul would agree. We tend to forget that the letters the apostle Paul wrote to churches are just that—letters to local communities of believers, and not just to me. It's also easy to overlook that Paul's letters to churches were written to people of different ethnicities and classes who had come together to form a multiethnic and multicultural community of faith. Paul was writing to Jews and Gentiles, rich and poor, slave and free, insiders and outsiders.

Hold on to this bit of context as Paul reminds the Ephesian church that they are "God's workmanship" (Ephesians 2:10). Can you see how these life-giving words would lift the heads of everyone, and particularly those who had found themselves on the lower rungs of first-century Roman society? Like James Brown's timely anthem, Paul's words in Ephesians 2:10 are laced with dignity. The word *workmanship* is one which conveys a message of value, of dignity. We weren't made merely by our biological parents, but by the sovereign, good purpose of God. Your mother and father may not have planned on you being here, but God did. You may have been called worthless. You may even feel worthless, but God says you're valuable. We are his workmanship.

This is a message we not only need to hear from God, but from each other. The project of human dignity is indeed best played as a team sport. While the organization Black Lives Matter has gathered well-earned controversy over the years, the message of black dignity should be anything but controversial. Black lives really do matter. What if we took the time to say it loud not just to ourselves, but to each other, that all people are of infinite value and worth, especially those who society has historically overlooked?

OLAUDAH "OXYMORON" EQUIANO

The Spirit of the Lord is upon me,
because he has anointed me
to proclaim good news to the poor.
He has sent me to proclaim liberty to the captives
and recovering of sight to the blind,
to set at liberty those who are oppressed,
to proclaim the year of the Lord's favor.

Luke 4:18-19

An oxymoron is something which on the surface of things appears to be a contradiction. The phrase "cruel kindness" is an oxymoron. And the phrase "black Christian" might seem like an oxymoron when we consider how many blacks were led to Christ by the very ones who enslaved them.

One of history's most profound oxymorons was Olaudah Equiano (c.1746–1797). At eleven, Olaudah and his sister were kidnapped from their home in Nigeria and sold to English slave traders, who would take them to Virginia. While he longed for freedom as a slave in America, Olaudah would hear his enslavers talk of another kind of freedom, a freedom of the soul which only Christ could provide. This too seemed to be an oxymoron—people who enslaved the body but believed in the emancipation of the soul.

Eventually, Olaudah earned his freedom and set sail for faraway places like the Caribbean, Turkey, and the Arctic Circle. During these voyages, he had plenty of time to reflect on the oxymoronic nature of these Christian enslavers. At the same time, he could not get away from the beauty of the gospel. He wrote, "Again, I was convinced that the Lord was better to me than I deserved . . . this mercy melted me down. When I considered my poor, wretched state, I wept, seeing what a great debtor I was to sovereign grace."[1] Olaudah became a follower of Jesus Christ.

His new faith, however, gave him no rest from the injustice of slavery, nor the gross contradiction of people who claimed to be committed to Christ and to injustice at the same time. The opposite, in fact—his belief in Jesus Christ compelled him to join the fight to end slavery. Olaudah picked up his pen and gave voice to his righteous rage, calling out the hypocrisy of people who both owned slaves and said they believed in Christ: "O, ye nominal Christians! Might not an African ask you, learned you this from your God?"[2]

Olaudah Equiano's autobiography became a bestseller, inspiring many in his new home of London to join the fight to abolish slavery. England abolished slavery, and several decades later, America would follow suit. Any black person today is indebted to Olaudah, for our freedoms can be traced back in part to his faith-fueled commitment to holistic emancipation—an emancipation of body and spirit, all inspired by the good news of Jesus Christ.

Olaudah's comprehensive understanding of the gospel as both being soul and body was inspired by his leader, Jesus Christ. In his first sermon, Jesus read from the prophet Isaiah and declared what God had sent him to do: "Proclaim good news to the poor . . . liberty to the captives and recovering of sight to the blind, to set at liberty those who are oppressed" (Luke 4:18). Over the years there has been much debate over the precise nature of Jesus' words in Luke 4. What exactly was Jesus referring to when he talked about the poor, the captive, and the blind? The spiritually poor, or the literally poor?

Was Jesus just talking of our souls, and freedom from sin? Or was Jesus talking about the marginalized of society? People who were in systems of oppression and beaten down by life economically? Was Jesus speaking of soul or body?

A glance at Jesus' ministry will answer this question. Of course there were times when Jesus talked of setting people spiritually free. Listen to Jesus preach as he calls people to turn from their sins, follow him, and enjoy spiritual life (e.g., Matthew 4:17). But we can scarcely turn the page in the Gospels and not find Jesus healing the physically infirm or feeding the hungry or rescuing people who had been harassed by life, providing much-needed physical and economic relief. The example of Jesus gives an emphatic "Yes! Both!" to the question of whether his ministry would set people free spiritually or physically.

Jesus was not an oxymoron who preached an emancipation of spirit yet provided no respite for oppressed bodies. The impulse of the gospel is to do everything we can to rescue spirit and body. The once-enslaved Olaudah Equiano got this. His educated enslavers, many of whom claimed Christianity, did not.

And what about us? Much has been said in recent years about critical race theory and woke ideology, so much that anyone invoking the very subject of race risks accusations of having capitulated to a political or ideological agenda. Real Christians, some would say, should be concerned with just sharing the gospel—as if the gospel has nothing to do with injustice of any kind, particularly racial injustice. But this is not the example Christ left us.

On the other side of the table—the receiving end—the gospel makes contradictions out of every black person in America, a country scarred by race. Every conversion is a miracle. But for black people like Olaudah to be saved after they were presented the gospel by the very ones who enslaved, tortured, raped, and sold off their children and families? They are oxymorons of the highest order. And in our day when racism continues to nip at our heels, "black Christian" remains an oxymoron, held together solely by the grip of God's grace.

THE DOZENS

And the king said, "Is there not still someone of the house of Saul, that I may show the kindness of God to him?" Ziba said to the king, "There is still a son of Jonathan; he is crippled in his feet."

2 Samuel 9:3

We called them "Yo Mama" jokes. We'd sit in our junior high cafeteria at lunch and throw insults at each other like we sometimes threw food:

"Yo mama so fat, her blood type is ragu!"

"Yo mama so old, she owes Moses a quarter!"

"Yo mama's house is so small, she has to go outside to change her mind!"

Please don't think less of me. I'm actually ashamed to admit we played this game—and not only because of the demeaning language. Around that table, it was only black people playing this game of trading insults that has historically been called "The Dozens."

The Dozens game has its origin in slavery.[1] When a slave was found to be mutilated, or to have some sort of physical or mental defect, they would be grouped by the dozens with other "defective" slaves to be sold on the auction block at a discounted price. They were literally cheaper by the dozen. Thus, to play the Dozens was to levy the worst kind of insult, for you were saying of the other person they were the lowest of the low, not even worthy of full price.

The gospel is at odds with this game we played. At its core, the gospel says that everyone is of value because everyone has been made in the image of God. This truth is scattered all over the Scriptures. When David becomes the second king of Israel, he asks, "Is there still anyone left of the house of Saul, that I may show him kindness for Jonathan's sake?" (2 Samuel 9:1). In that culture, people would have found David's inquiry odd. Sure, new kings asked if there was anyone left of the old regime, but it wasn't so they could show kindness to them; it was so they could kill them and put an end to the competition.

By this point King Saul had died, along with his son Jonathan, David's best friend. David was grief stricken over the death of his friend. Remembering his covenant with Jonathan, this newly crowned King of Israel wanted to bless his house (1 Samuel 18:1-4). So they found a son of Jonathan . . . a crippled son named Mephibosheth. Instead of killing him, David invited him to eat at the table with him and instructed his servants to make sure Mephibosheth's home was always provided for. Mephibosheth could not believe what he had just heard. He thought he was being called in to be killed, not to be blessed. "So Mephibosheth lived in Jerusalem, for he ate always at the king's table. Now he was lame in both his feet" (2 Samuel 9:13).

Every time I read this story I'm moved. How kind can someone be, right? I mean, it makes me want to go out and be like David, find someone who has some sort of need and bless them. That's a worthy application of the story, but I don't think that's the primary point.

David is a type of Christ, who, motivated by covenantal love, invites a person deemed unworthy to eat forever at his table. This is the gospel story. Christ is the true and better David, and we are Mephibosheth—people who have been disabled by sin, deserving of death. We must come to terms with how sin has deformed us all, making us a part of the world's Dozens. We're all in need of a Savior who bought us not at a discount, but at infinite cost to himself. Until we realize this, we will look down with contempt on those we deem to be Mephibosheth.

Lose touch with your inner Mephibosheth, and we leave the door cracked for arrogance and pride to creep in.

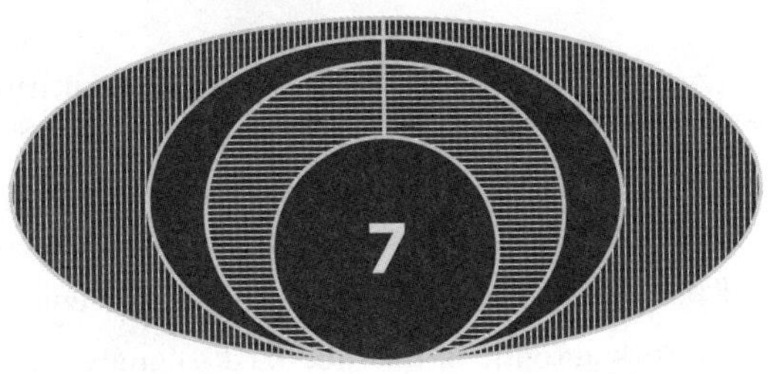

7

THE FATHER OF MODERN GAMING

The LORD said to Moses, "See, I have called by name Bezalel the son of Uri, son of Hur of the tribe of Judah, and I have filled him with the Spirit of God, with ability and intelligence, with knowledge and all craftsmanship, to devise artistic designs."

EXODUS 31:1-4

I have a confession to make, and I hope this is a safe place: I love the video game Pac-Man. I don't mean I used to love it. I *still* love it. I'll just go ahead and out myself. When you see me on my phone in the middle of a particularly boring meeting, I'm not taking notes or reading the Bible. I'm just trying to get to the next level on my Pac-Man app. It's a throwback to my youth, when one afternoon over at my friend Skeeter's house I was introduced to Atari and all the different games.

Little did I know I was benefiting from the handiwork of a black man named Jerry Lawson (1940–2011), a self-made engineer from Queens, New York and one of the first black engineers in what has come to be called Silicon Valley. Known as the "father of modern gaming," Lawson helped to invent the first video game console with interchangeable game cartridges.[1] That's right: without his invention there would be no Atari, Nintendo, Sega, PlayStation, or Xbox. Chances are that if you or anyone in your home is a young adult or younger, you have some sort of video game system whose roots go back to Jerry Lawson.

It's easy for Christians to belittle the contributions of people like Lawson, since most of us have been handed a worldview that says some types of work are more important than others. *Surely inventing the system for video games is not on par with a pastor's calling, or doing the Lord's work*, many have been taught to think. This framework of sacred versus secular is at odds with the Bible. Not only does God see all work that contributes to the betterment of society as good, but he is himself the giver of the very gifts which enable a person to do their work.

The opening verses of Exodus 31 are instructive, as we hear God telling Moses how he has given Bezalel gifts of craftmanship and artistic designs for the constructing of his tabernacle. Bezalel wasn't the only one to receive these particular gifts. God would go on to tell Moses, "I have given to all able men ability, that they may make all that I have commanded you" (Exodus 31:6). (And where you read "men," think of all people.) Or as James says, "Every good gift and every perfect gift is from above, coming down from the Father of lights" (James 1:17).

Think of how dull, lifeless, and intolerable our world would be without artists. How boring it would be without people endowed with gifts of creativity, good and perfect gifts given to them by a God who takes great delight in redemptive expression! It was God, after all, who greenlighted Adam to name the animals. I can see God laughing from a place of deep joy as Adam gives names like "orangutan" and "praying mantis." And I can also see God shaking his head as Adam, clearly in a rush to get home after a very long day of naming animals, gives out less original names: "Cat. Bat. Rat. Gnat."

While I ask for your forgiveness in letting my imagination get the best of me, the truth is that God has graced our world with creatives like Bezalel and Jerry Lawson. What's more, if I read Exodus 31 right, God made sure to make a place for these artists to let their imaginations roam. They worked with great skill on the very place where God would be worshipped. This should be instructive for our churches today. We need to make room for artists to use their gifts for the glory of God and our good.

But artistry should not be limited to the local church. I don't know what you do for a living, but what I do know is that we need exponentially more people in the marketplace who love Jesus, work with great skill, and who see their abilities and jobs as gifts and callings from God.

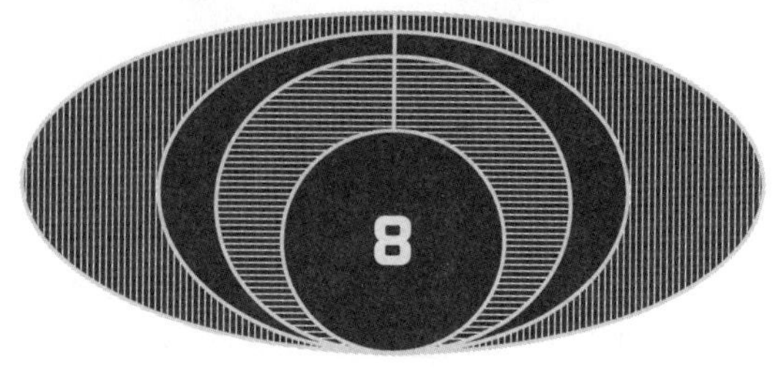

BILLIE HOLIDAY AND HER "STRANGE FRUIT"

If I say, "I will not mention him,
or speak any more in his name,"
there is in my heart as it were a burning fire
shut up in my bones,
and I am weary with holding it in,
and I cannot.

JEREMIAH 20:9

She was fine as long as she stuck with safe songs like "God Bless the Child." But the moment she started singing the protest song "Strange Fruit," she crossed over from entertainer to prophet, from pet to threat. The white establishment was in no mood to hear a song about lynching. Billie was crooning of "Black bodies swinging in the southern breeze, strange fruit hanging from the poplar trees."

We love the song now, but Billie Holiday (1915–1959) was singing far before the civil rights movement. She had the courage to sing this song in the late 1930s. "Courage" is the right word, because when the government told her to remove the song permanently from her set, she stiffened her back and refused. For Billie not to use her gift to sing out against injustice would itself have been a form of injustice.

Little did she know her courage would have fatal consequences.

Billie Holiday's refusal to comply brought about the ire of Harry J. Anslinger, head of the Federal Bureau of Narcotics. Harry was looking for an angle to exact revenge on Billie for her defiance, and when he became aware of Billie Holiday's drug use, he had just the excuse he needed.[1]

Harry Anslinger cared nothing of the *why* behind Billie's addiction. The fact she was raped at the age of ten and forced to work in a brothel with her mother when she was a preteen, where for three years she endured the constant sexual assaults of men, meant nothing to him. Nor did Harry express any empathy for Billie at the abuse she endured from her husband, who beat her body so badly she had to get her ribs taped to perform. Just the opposite. Harry Anslinger decided to use Billie Holiday's husband to get evidence of her addiction, securing her arrest. In state's custody, and in severe withdrawal from her addiction, Billie was handcuffed to her hospital bed where she died on July 17, 1959, of heart failure. She was just forty-four.

Her life would have been so much easier had she kept her mouth shut and stopped with all the "Strange Fruit" business. But it's really hard for me to believe that given another chance Billie would have done things differently.

The prophet Jeremiah's life would have been a lot smoother had he, too, stopped crooning about injustice. Over the years, the black church has found comfort in his words. In haunting similarity with Billie Holiday, Jeremiah could not see injustice and keep his mouth shut. If he had, he would have imploded, since "there is in my heart as it were a burning fire shut up in my bones, and I am weary with holding it in, and I cannot" (Jeremiah 20:9). So Jeremiah went on rant after prophetic rant, calling out the injustice around him. This did not win him any popularity contests. Instead he found himself, like Billie Holiday, in state custody, thrown into a pit, wronged by the power structures of his time.

Martin Luther King Jr. famously observed that the moral arc of the universe is long, but it bends toward justice.[2] While his observation aligns with the Christian worldview, the testimony of the prophet Jeremiah and the prophetess Billie Holiday would dispel any notion that justice will always come in our lifetime. Long after he died, Jeremiah's Israel would make it through the dark night of their soul, be rescued from their Babylonian exile, and see the coming of the Messiah. And it would be in 2022, well over a half century after Billie's death, when an anti-lynching bill, known as the Emmett Till Anti-Lynching Act, would be passed into law, putting the strange fruit of black bodies "hanging from poplar trees" on the extinction list.

The witness of history is that justice will come. God will have the final say. We may not see it in our lifetime, but there will come a day when the accounts of justice will be settled.

But what are we to do in the meantime, as we see people trafficked for sex and women assaulted everywhere from college campuses to casting couches? How are we to respond to police brutality, unlivable wages, workplace discrimination, school shootings, the slaughter of unborn babies, the circumstances and systems that put women in the position to even contemplate such horrors, and countless more injustices? The people of God cannot let Jeremiah's fire go out. We must do whatever we can to nurture the embers in our own hearts, so we are compelled to sing background to Billie's call for justice.

There is a cost, however, when we cry out for justice—just as there is a cost when we shrink back in silence. And this cost is particularly high when it comes to blacks singing out against injustice. When Harry Anslinger found out about the actress Judy Garland's drug addiction, he flew out to meet with her. While they were together, Harry encouraged Judy to take a long vacation and get some rest. Judy was afforded this privilege because she was white and posed no threat to the establishment. Not so with Billie and many other blacks. To be black and to sing for justice has always been a dangerous game. We run the risk of crossing over from pet to threat.

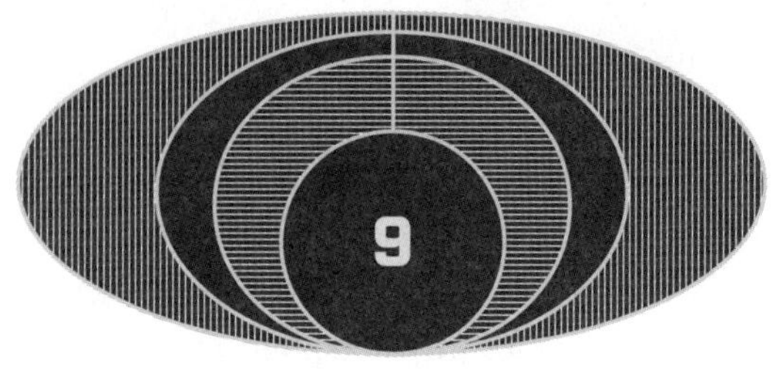

NOT TODAY

Shadrach, Meshach, and Abednego answered and said to the king, "O Nebuchadnezzar, we have no need to answer you in this matter. If this be so, our God whom we serve is able to deliver us from the burning fiery furnace, and he will deliver us out of your hand, O king. But if not, be it known to you, O king, that we will not serve your gods, or worship the golden image that you have set up."

DANIEL 3:16-18

History tends to turn on little acts of defiance. They are what I like to call "not-today" moments. It's a group of people saying "Not today!" as they toss tea into the Boston Harbor. It's a tired Rosa Parks saying, "Not today" when told to give up her seat. And it's a nineteen-year-old David Isom, in St. Petersburg, Florida, who just casually jumps into a swimming pool in defiance of the cultural norms of his time.

In 1957, St. Petersburg, under intense legal pressure, had desegregated its swimming pool. But everyone knew those were just words. Business went on as usual, with black people continuing their inconvenient trek from St. Petersburg to Tampa Bay if they wanted to swim.

On June 8, 1958, things changed. David Isom (1939–1970) purchased his ticket, walked into the all-white Spa Pool, took off his shirt, and jumped into the cool water. Around fifty shocked whites took in the scene, got out of the pool, toweled off, and left in disgust. Isom enjoyed the pool for about an hour before making his way back home. David's actions led to the closure of the pool for the next week. But in 1959, Spa Pool truly became more than legally desegregated.

Blacks no longer caravanned out to Tampa; they chose instead to follow Isom's lead. When asked why he took such a bold, culture-defying dive that June day, Isom said, "I just feel that it's not a privilege to use the pool, but a right."[1]

Thank you, David, for teaching us that if we want tomorrow to change, we have to begin by saying "Not today" to the status quo.

The story of Shadrach, Meshach, and Abednego's defiance in the book of Daniel has long held a special place in the heart of the black church. Fresh from a dream where he sees a large image, the king now decides to have one constructed and commands everyone to bow in worship of his idol. When the music cues them to bow, everyone does as they are told—except for three young men, who hold their own not-today moment. They refuse to go along with the status quo.

When word gets back to the king of their rebellion, he calls them in for a closed-door meeting where he gives them one more opportunity to bend to his wishes. If they refuse, the king warns, they will be thrown into the fiery furnace. As cool as David Isom was that June day, taking off his shirt and jumping into the all-white pool, these young men dig their heels in and offer a final word of defiance: "Be it known to you, O king, that we will not serve your gods or worship the golden image that you have set up" (Daniel 3:18). Furious, the king commands the furnace be heated seven times hotter and has them thrown in.

But they don't burn. God shows up and delivers them as the king looks on in awe. One chapter later, the king bows in worship not to his own image, but to the King of kings and Lord of lords. Shadrach, Meshach, and Abednego's not-today moment proved catalytic in changing the heart of the king.

And what about you? What do you need to say "Not today" to? What act of God-glorifying defiance do you need to perform? Maybe it's saying "Not today" to a certain relationship. Or "Not today" to the pressures to compromise your sexual integrity. Or "Not today" to a quick temper and impatience. Or "Not today" to patterns of disrespect you have endured from certain people in your life.

Defiance has a way of waving goodbye to the status quo, and hello to a brighter future.

10

INVALUABLY HIDDEN

But God has so composed the body, giving greater honor to the part that lacked it.

1 Corinthians 12:24

You have to make a choice, okay? Like, *have* to. If someone comes to you and says, "Give me either your mouth or your liver," which one are you going to part with? While I'm pretty confident I know your answer, give it some thought. We will come back to the question.

Of course, you know the name Martin Luther King Jr. How could you not? There are around a thousand streets named after him in the United States. He has a national holiday and monument in our nation's capital. But if I asked you about Wyatt Tee Walker (1929–2018), his name would not register with most people in our country—and that is a real shame. Dr. Walker was Martin Luther King Jr.'s first chief of staff, from 1960–1964; he was the brains behind the civil rights movement. That's right, there's no Birmingham campaign (1963) without Walker. There's no March on Washington with King's iconic "I Have a Dream" speech (1963) without Walker. And a good case could be that made King wouldn't have won the Nobel Prize (1964) without several years of sheer behind-the-scenes administrative genius conducted by Walker, freeing his boss to inspire and lead the masses.

If they were parts of the body, King would be the mouth and Walker would be the liver.

One of Paul's frustrations when he addresses the Corinthians is their fascination with the "mouths" of society; you know, the really impressive orators of the day. Those who could turn a phrase like none other, gather a crowd, and gain a following. While Paul would spend significant time on this matter in his second letter to the Corinthians, we get a hint of his frustration in his first letter. Paul spends chapters twelve through fourteen reminding Christ-followers of our value when he uses the image of the body and the role each of us plays. The body, Paul states, is diverse, filled with different parts. The problem is that we tend to honor the parts we do see and ignore the parts we don't. In fact, the parts we don't see are often more valuable than the ones we do see.

So let me ask you again: If you had to part with either your mouth or your liver, which one would you say goodbye to? You can live without your mouth. Yeah, we'd have to figure out another way to get nutrients into your body, and you wouldn't be able to talk, but you could still communicate. But take away your liver, and you have no shot at life.

We see and hear mouths all day long. Unless you are in the medical profession, chances are you won't see a liver today. The parts we don't see are more valuable than the ones we do see.

I'm thankful we don't have to make that choice, but do you see Paul's point? Like the culture of the Corinthians, we live in a world where the orators—the mouths—get all the attention, while the Wyatt Tee Walkers rarely get their flowers. That is just a real shame, because without him, the freedoms I enjoy as a black man would not have happened.

Do you feel hidden? Ignored? Overlooked? Do you feel as if you haven't received the credit or the accolades you're due? God sees, and he's chosen to give you gifts and position you in an irreplaceable section of his body. And if you're a leader, someone out front, do all you can to celebrate your liver, because you cannot function without it.

If you ever get tired of being unknown or overlooked, look to Dr. Wyatt Tee Walker and be encouraged.

11

ZIPPORAH'S HOT COMB

Miriam and Aaron spoke against Moses because of the Cushite woman whom he had married, for he had married a Cushite woman.

NUMBERS 12:1

There's a popular warning when it comes to interracial relationships told over the years, especially involving black and white couples with contrasting hair textures: "If they can't use your comb, don't bring them home."

The Douglass family found this out the hard way.

On a January morning in 1884, the most famous man of the nineteenth century married the daughter of a highly influential upstate New York family (the wedding was officiated by the well-known black Presbyterian pastor Francis Grimké, the namesake of Grimké

Seminary). His name was Frederick Douglass. Her name was Helen Pitts. He was black. She was white. They had become acquainted through her abolitionist parents, who not only cheered their feminist daughter on and gloried in her work as a schoolteacher to black students but also threw themselves into ending slavery. But when they discovered she had married a black man they drew a hard line, disowning Helen and writing her out of their will. (Much later, her mother would warm to the union.)[1]

Wait a minute. A racist abolitionist? Yep. A racist liberal? Yep. A racist Christian? Yes again.

But let's not rush to cancel Mr. and Mrs. Pitts. They are hardly the only ones to resist a family member's choice of a mate. In the book of Numbers, we see another family express outrage over an interracial relationship. We know Moses, but many are not acquainted with his African wife, Zipporah. Notice the redundancy of Numbers 12:1: "Miriam and Aaron spoke against Moses because of the Cushite woman whom he had married, for he had married a Cushite." You don't have to spend a day in seminary learning all of the fancy linguistics to see what's going on here. The author is clearly underscoring Moses' choice of a spouse, and the fact she is from Cush. Where is Cush? Good question. It's in Northern Africa.

That's right, Moses married an African. A black woman. A woman whose hair may have been of such a particular texture that what we now call a hot comb may have been needed.

She may not have been able to use Moses' comb, but he brought her home anyway, and his sister Miriam and brother Aaron didn't like it one bit. They were so disgusted with Moses' decision they decided to call a family meeting to unload. Bad mistake, because a few verses later, God shows up, and he is not a happy camper. His words and actions are worth quoting in full:

> And the LORD came down in a pillar of cloud and stood at the entrance of the tent and called Aaron and Miriam, and they both came forward. And he said, "Hear my words: If there is a prophet among you, I the LORD make myself known to him in a vision; I speak with him in a dream. Not so with my servant Moses. He is faithful in all my house. With him I speak mouth to mouth, clearly, and not in riddles, and he beholds the form of the LORD. Why then were you not afraid to speak against my servant Moses?" And the anger of the LORD was kindled against them, and he departed.
>
> When the cloud removed from over the tent, behold, Miriam was leprous, like snow. (Numbers 12:5-10)

Funny, not funny.

I say that because of the irony of making Miriam "leprous, like snow." The imagery of color has been a theme in our text. The name "Cush" is not just a reference to Zipporah's country of origin, but it also has color connotations, as the name means "black." Miriam is in all likelihood lighter than her sister-in-law, and finds her identity in her color. So God, in one of history's tragic ironies, says in so many words, "You like being bright? Well, I can make you brighter," and she becomes leprous, "like snow."

But there's a deeper irony. At the time, as Israel was making her way through the wilderness to the Promised Land, when a person contracted leprosy, they were considered social outcasts and had to be removed to outside of the camp. To be a leper was to be an outsider, far away from God and the presence of community. Miriam thinks she's the insider. She treats Zipporah with contempt, looking down on her as if she is the outsider. In a flash, God flips the script, making Miriam the outsider, while Zipporah remains the insider.

Do you see what God is doing here? Our status has nothing to do with the pigmentation of our skin and the unfortunate cultural connotations which come along with color. Being in or out is all about our relationship with God. We all were outsiders; sin has made lepers of us all, cast far away from God. But on the cross, Jesus Christ died for the sins of the world, bringing us near to the God who made us.

This is a truth I hope Helen's parents came to terms with. It's a truth we still need to hear today. For far too many "Christians" are fine with being your brother in Christ, just not your brother-in-law.

BLACK EXCELLENCE

And there was an Ethiopian, a eunuch, a court official of Candace, queen of the Ethiopians, who was in charge of all her treasure. He had come to Jerusalem to worship and was returning, seated in his chariot, and he was reading the prophet Isaiah.

Acts 8:27-28

"Hurry up! The show is about to come on!"

If you were born, as my kids used to say, in the "Nineteens," you remember saying those words. Long before we could pause our television sets or watch TV on demand, long before we had all of these streaming services with all of this content within arm's reach to watch any time we wanted, the average American household only had a handful of channels.

This was the era of network television, when CBS, ABC, and NBC ruled the airwaves. These were the days when you couldn't wait to get to school the next day to talk to your friends about last night's episode, because you just knew they all had watched the same thing you had, at the same time.

Ahh, the good old days.

On September 24, 1987, *A Different World* premiered. It was a spinoff from *The Cosby Show* and followed daughter Denise Huxtable as she made her way from Brooklyn to the fictitious Hillman College, a school that was portrayed as part of the network of historically black colleges and universities (HBCUs).

For six seasons, Thursday nights and *A Different World* were sacred in black homes. My friends and I would debate who was more beautiful, Denise or Whitley. We wondered when geeky Dwayne would get together with diva Whitley. We learned about reclaiming "Mammy," and watched people who looked like us taking their education seriously. And we also saw the show take on the cultural issues of the late twentieth century, issues like the AIDS crisis and the Los Angeles riots, which were instigated by the beating of a black Rodney King at the merciless hands of white police officers.

Not long after the LA riots, the show ended. But before Mr. and Mrs. Wayne (yes, Dwayne and Whitley finally married) took off for their own different world, along with the rest of the cast in the final episode, *A Different World* had made its mark. One study revealed that from the mid-1970s to the 1990s, enrollment in HBCUs had increased by 26 percent—and the six years that the television show was on accounted for "virtually all" of that uptick in attendance.[1] How could it not? Seeing black excellence on college campuses week in and week out gave me and my friends a vision for what could be.

Like the weekly scenes at fictitious Hillman College, the Acts 8 scene of an Ethiopian man reading the Bible has long inspired black people. This man is not only from Africa, but is a man of importance; as Luke points out, he is "a court official of Candace" (Acts 8:27). And when we meet him, he's not playing sports or talking trash or trying to hit on a woman. He's reading. It's not that reading was special for a black person; back then, to see *anyone* reading would have been unusual, as literacy rates at the time are estimated to be around ten percent.[2] And what is he reading? The Bible.

Philip takes all of this in, a conversation ensues, and this man is led to faith in Jesus Christ. And according to church history, he goes back to his home in Africa and lays the foundation for what would become a major gospel movement, with the Ethiopian Orthodox Church tracing its roots back to him. Long before Christianity was popularized by Constantine and swept through Europe, it gained a foothold in Africa.

And people say Christianity is a white man's religion.

Black people come from a long lineage of excellence. Our history is filled with men and women who were educated, took their faith seriously, and made positive contributions to their world. Their example inspired others.

To be black in America is often to be unduly burdened with the expectations of a community looking to you to represent them well. Every "first" or "close-to-first" has felt this pressure, from Jackie

Robinson to Condoleezza Rice to Barack Obama. But on the other hand, we rightly bear a responsibility to inspire others through our hard work and commitment to excellence. We owe it to others to live in such a way those who come behind us see the possibilities for what could be.

I had my Hillman College shirt on the other day when a white woman stopped to tell me that one of her friends attended there. She said it with such kindness and conviction, I didn't have the heart to tell her she was confused. I played along and asked when her friend graduated, and watched her struggle to recall. As we walked away, I chuckled a bit (as the English say, I can be a bit cheeky), and then thought to myself about how I wish Hillman was a real place. If it were, I'd make a point to go to a graduation or crash an alumni function so I could thank Dwayne, Whitley, Denise, Kim, and the entire class for showing me what could be.

A MOMENT OF SILENCE FOR ANARCHA, LUCY, AND BETSEY

They were stoned, they were sawn in two, they were killed with the sword. They went about in skins of sheep and goats, destitute, afflicted, mistreated—of whom the world was not worthy—wandering about in deserts and mountains, and in dens and caves of the earth.

And all these, though commended through their faith, did not receive what was promised, since God had provided something better for us, that apart from us they should not be made perfect.

Hebrews 11:37-40

If you're a woman, the next time you go to see the gynecologist, whisper a word of thanks for Anarcha, Lucy, and Betsey.

In the 1840s, J. Marion Sims moved into the slave-trading district of Montgomery, Alabama, to set up his practice, where he pioneered his gynecological techniques on enslaved women without any form of pain medication. His work did bear some fruit, as Sims developed a treatment for fistulas (I'll spare you the details), which required these women to endure at least an hourlong, extremely painful surgery.

We do not know how many slaves he experimented on, but we know it was a lot. Sims once reflected, "There was never a time that I could not at any day have a subject for operation."[1] Sims never lacked for a "subject" because slaveowners needed their property to be able to reproduce, providing an ample return on their investment. If there was any question, any delay to the ability of their slaves to have offspring, off to Sims they went. Yet for all of Sim's "subjects," he only took the time to write down three of their names—Anarcha, Lucy, and Betsey.

Once Sims perfected his experiments on black women, he moved onto white women, who were given pain medication to withstand the surgery.

In 1876, Sims was elected president of the American Medical Association. And four years later he became the president of the American Gynecological Society, where he was widely regarded as the "father of gynecology." Statues have been made in honor of Sims. And as a matter of full disclosure, ladies, if you ever go in for surgery they very well may use an instrument named after him called the Sims retractor.

All of this at the expense of black women.

Where was God when Anarcha, Lucy, and Betsey had their legs thrust open and were performed on, as I'm sure the tears trickled down their faces as they whispered their prayers? Surely God heard the many screams that crashed through the doors of Sims's practice. If I'm honest, it seems that God is passive too many times. For the life of me, I have trouble with a God who has it in his power to remove evil but chooses not to. In these dark moments I find comfort in Hebrews 11.

If you haven't taken the time to read Hebrews chapter 11 in its entirety, you should. You'll find much of it to be inspiring, as you hear stories of victorious faith. Stories of Noah and his ark. Stories of Abraham and Moses. Stories of women who were infertile, prayed to God and God did something about it. Stories of people who believed God in the face of the impossible, and saw God work miracles.

But keep reading and you'll see the chapter take a turn from victorious faith to legacy faith. While there are plenty of people in the Bible who saw God do what they prayed for, there is a whole cast of others who prayed and prayed—and then God *did not* show up the way they hoped. God seemed passive. Biblical history is littered with men and women who were killed for their faith in Christ, with many of them begging God to deliver them, and God said and did nothing. And then there's Jesus. On the night he was betrayed, he went into the Garden of Gethsemane and asked God to provide another means for his death. God said no.

This seems more than strange, doesn't it? Is God really being passive or flippant? No. The writer of Hebrews says God's silence is never cruel passivity but is a part of a grand plan that includes you and me and generations to come. Look at what the writer says of those who did not get what they had hoped for from God: "And all these, though commended through their faith, did not receive what was promised, since God had provided something better for us" (Hebrews 11:39-40).

Here the writer of Hebrews helps to enlarge our perspective. God, the writer argues, cannot be judged based on what does or does not happen in my lifetime. We are finite beings bound by space and time; God is infinite with no boundaries. We tend to see ourselves as disconnected individuals; God sees us as connected communally and intergenerationally.

My great-great-grandfather Peter was a slave in North Carolina. He was a man of faith. Do you think he ever prayed for equality? I'm sure he did, but he never saw it. He's in heaven now looking down on his great-great-grandson writing books and leading a movement to see the multiethnic church become the new normal in society. Do you know how many times I've climbed into bed in some hotel in some faraway town after I preached to a diverse audience about biblical justice and thought of my great-great-grandfather Peter? I'm the fulfillment of his prayers. He never saw it, but, boy, am I living out what he begged God for. That's legacy faith.

And then there's my sister, a black woman you should address as Dr. Holly Gibson. She's a gynecologist, providing great care to her patients in a profession that at one time cared nothing for her. Every time Holly—I mean, Dr. Gibson—walks into her office or goes to perform surgery, I imagine Anarcha, Betsey, and Lucy looking down from heaven, covering their mouths in delight, to try to keep from eking out a different kind of scream—a joyful scream. "Only God," they must be thinking. Dr. Gibson is an answer to their prayers.

What has gone unanswered in your life? What are you frustrated with God about? Have you been praying about griefs and longings which seem more than reasonable, but all you are getting from God is silence? If there's one thing we know from Hebrews 11 and the witness of history, it's that God's silence is never apathy or passivity. He very well may give you the answer you are looking for in your lifetime. Or he may be thinking about your great-great-grandchildren, who will enjoy the answer to your prayers. Keep praying. Keep believing.

EDWARD'S CROSSOVER

To the Jews I became as a Jew, in order to win Jews. . . . To those outside the law I became as one outside the law. . . . I do it all for the sake of the gospel, that I may share with them in its blessings.

1 Corinthians 9:20-23

My pastor, Dr. Kenneth Ulmer, is a legendary storyteller, and one of his favorite stories is about the time he—a young black pastor of a growing Los Angeles congregation—got to tag along with *the* Dr. Edward Victor Hill (1933–2003). Dr. Hill had just preached the paint off the walls at the National Baptist Convention annual meeting in the Midwest, one of the largest gatherings of black Christians.

They walked off stage and rushed to the car; they had to get across town so that Dr. Hill could fulfill another speaking commitment, this one at a large conservative white evangelical school. But he was hungry, so they stopped at some joint to grab a quick bite. As they waited on their food, Dr. Hill removed a pen from his coat pocket and began writing on a napkin. My pastor asked him what he was going to preach at this college. Dr. Hill said he was figuring it out right then and right there on that napkin.

Well, they got to the college and, once again, Dr. Hill preached the paint off the walls. They got back in the car after a full day, and my pastor could no longer contain himself. He had just witnessed Dr. Hill destroy a black convention and a conservative white college in the same day, all while being his authentic self. "How did you do that?" my pastor asked.

"Kenny," said Dr. Hill, "you have to preach a gospel big enough for National Baptists and conservative white evangelicals."

No discussion of great preaching in general, and certainly great black preachers, is complete without a significant look at the life and ministry of Pastor Edward Victor Hill. He pastored the Mount Zion Missionary Baptist Church in Los Angeles and was known among the preaching fraternity as a preacher's preacher, with his gift being so large it allowed him to cross over and traffic in eclectic circles.

Dr. Hill was close friends with Jerry Falwell Sr. (founder of Liberty University and one of the architects of the Moral Majority) and gave the opening prayer at Richard Nixon's second inauguration. When President George H. W. Bush came to town, he stopped by Dr. Hill's church. But just when you thought he was a Republican, Dr. Hill endorsed his friend Jesse Jackson's 1984 bid for president, to the ire of his conservative friends.

And talk about his friends. Pastor Hill was close to the morally fallen like Jim Bakker and Jimmy Swaggart, refusing to turn his back on them at their lowest moments. But he was also friends with moral models like Billy Graham. Dr. Hill defied labels, leaving you to wonder what to make of him. Dr. Hill would simply say, "Call me a follower of Jesus and a preacher of the gospel."

So would Paul. Have you paid attention to the eclectic environments Paul trafficked in, or his diverse circle of friends? In Athens you could find him in the synagogue with Jews one day, and up on Mars Hill with the Greek philosophers the next. And in his first letter to the Corinthians, Paul relishes in his diverse friendships. He tells them that his decision to be inclusive was not motivated by an ideological agenda, but by a gospel greed to see people from all walks of life, cultures, and ethnicities hear the good news of Jesus Christ (1 Corinthians 9:19-23). Paul, too, preached a gospel big enough for Baptists and Presbyterians and more.

But let's not rush to conclude that Paul and Dr. Hill were ashamed of how God made them or rejected their ethnicity. Absolutely not. Dr. Hill was very proud of his black preaching tradition; he brought his full embodied self into the preaching moment. He just refused to make his blackness the punchline of his life. Listen to what he says:

> I don't know anything about a white Christ—I know about Christ, a Savior named Jesus. I don't know what color He is. He was born in brown Asia, He fled to black Africa, and He was in heaven before the gospel got to white Europe, so I don't

> know what color He is. I do know one thing: if you bow at the altar with color on your mind, and get up with color on your mind, go back again—and keep going back until you no longer look at His color, but at His greatness and His power—His power to save![1]

And what about you? What's the most important thing in your life? What drives you? Is it the gospel of Jesus Christ? And what about your dinner table, or network of friends? Do you, like Paul and Dr. Hill, traffic in eclectic circles? Sure, color and ethnicity and culture should have their place. We should never dismiss these things, since we have intentionally been made embodied beings in the image of God. But may our core be found not in our color or culture, but in our Christ.

COOKIES AND CAGED BIRDS

And the twelve were with him, and also some women who had been healed of evil spirits and infirmities: Mary, called Magdalene.

Luke 8:1-2

In 1969, Maya Angelou (1928–2014) released her memoir *I Know Why the Caged Bird Sings*. For the next two years, it would occupy the *New York Times* bestseller list. The book has never gone out of print; it has sold over a million copies and has been translated into seventeen different languages.

Maya Angelou was born Marguerite Johnson in Stamps, Arkansas. At the age of seven she was raped by her mother's boyfriend. Unable to process her trauma, she shut down and became the town mute. No one could get to her, not even her mother. Enter Mrs. Flowers, the most adored woman in Stamps. She invited young Marguerite over for some tea and cookies. This kindness turned into a weekly ritual. Slowly, Marguerite began to speak.[1]

Before it was all said and done, she had written several books, acted, produced, served on the front lines of the civil rights movement, and taught at prestigious universities. That's right, "Mute Marguerite" would go on to become wordsmith Maya, whose speeches commanded thousands of dollars and whose words touched millions of lives.

All from a little tea and cookies.

A little kindness goes a long way. We see this in Luke 8, where Luke is careful to point out a woman named Mary who, like young Marguerite, had endured trauma. Turns out Mary Magdalene had been oppressed by seven demons. Jesus, in a display of kindness, cast the demons out of her. Mary's life would be transformed by his kindness. She would go on to follow Jesus all the way to the cross as his disciples fled.

On the day of the resurrection, Mary was among the first who went to the tomb to bring spices for Jesus' body (Matthew 28:1; Mark 16:1). When she found the tomb empty, she ran to tell Peter and John (John 20:2). Jesus would go on to tell Mary to tell his followers he would ascend to heaven (John 20:17). She obeyed and reported to them, "I have seen the Lord" (John 20:18). What turned Mary from a social outsider to a spiritual insider and first eyewitness to the greatest miracle in human history? A little "tea and cookies" from

Jesus. If kindness were an airline traveler, it would have elite status—it goes a really long way.

And what about you? Who around you is in need of a little tea and cookies? Where are your Marguerite Johnsons? Your Mary Magdalenes? In our busy, smartphone-distracted, work-obsessed world, may we stop long enough to show kindness to those who've hit a rough stretch. Who knows, they may become our next Maya Angelou.

MICHAEL TAKES ON MTV

And when they began to sing and praise, the LORD set an ambush against the men of Ammon, Moab, and Mount Seir, who had come against Judah, so that they were routed.

2 CHRONICLES 20:22

On the evening of February 27, 1980, Michael Joseph Jackson (1958–2009) won the Grammy award for best R&B vocal performance, male, for his song "Don't Stop Till You Get Enough," from his album *Off the Wall.*

His happiness was short-lived.

It's not that he had been nominated for two Grammys but only received one. Michael's disappointment lay in the fact his album had been burdened with limitations. There was something about the label "R&B" that unsettled him. Don't misunderstand Michael. He loved and respected rhythm and blues. How could he not? He worshipped James Brown, even incorporating the "Godfather of Soul's" signature dance moves in his audition for Motown. But as Michael grew as an artist, so did his vision. And to get where he was going, Michael needed to be free.

So back to the studio he went with his producer from *Off the Wall*, Quincy Jones. When they were finished, they presented to the world the number-one-selling album of all time: *Thriller*. You just can't overstate the success of this album. Each single that was released reached the top ten of the Billboard 100. He won an astounding eight Grammys. To date, the album has sold over one hundred million copies and exceeds over two and a half billion streams a year.

Yes, that's *billion*, with a "B."

History often happens at the crossroads of giftedness and opportunity. Nowhere is this truer than with Michael Jackson. His ascendancy coincides with the emergence of the music video. Don't get me wrong: if *Thriller* released today, it would still be a classic. What Michael and Quincy gave us was timeless beauty. But with music videos not being now what they were in the late twentieth century, I'm not so sure *Thriller* would have been today what it was back then. And that leads us to the problem. Take a deep breath and let this sink in: MTV (yes, they actually played music videos all the time then, believe it or not) wasn't really trying to put Michael, or any black artist, on their programming. They masked their racism by saying they were a rock and roll outlet. But after the CEO of Michael's label threatened to pull his white artists from MTV, they opened the door, and there was Michael, first in line.

On March 31, 1983, "Beat It" premiered on MTV (a few weeks before this, his hit "Billie Jean" debuted). Can't you see Michael in his iconic red Beat It jacket with all those zippers? His choice of song was a perfect fit for MTV given the guitar solo. When you coupled this with its urban street themes and his dance moves, audiences weren't quite sure how to label Jackson—which is exactly what he wanted. And then, in December of 1983, his single "Thriller" had its coming-out party on MTV. While the average video during that time cost around fifty thousand dollars, Michael paid over a million to make "Thriller." It turned out to be money well spent, as Michael gave us something we had never experienced before—a musical short film. MTV played so much Michael Jackson, it was joked that the "M" in MTV stood for "Michael."

And thus, the proverbial floodgates were opened to black artists, and other genres of music. Soon came *Yo! MTV Raps*, *MTV Jams*, and then *Pimp My Ride*, hosted by a black, cornrow-wearing rap artist named Xzibit! And to think Michael started it all.

Music has always possessed a unique ability to break glass ceilings and destroy barriers. And I don't just mean the barriers of race or class; I believe in spiritual barriers as well. When I preach, I always prefer to speak after praise and worship. The few times I've taught before the music has felt like . . . well, like I was trying to drive my car with the emergency brake on. Music shifts things. It changes things. It breaks things up and pioneers new paths.

This is what we see in 2 Chronicles 20, where the nation of Israel has been given the news of a large army coming against them. As they gather to pray and fast, the Lord gives unique instructions. When they go out into battle, they are not to put the infantry in front, with their best marksmen. Instead, they are to position the praise team first, who would lead them into battle with song. If ever I were tempted to say, "I don't know about this one, God," this would be the time.

But the people do as instructed. The praise team sings and worships their way onto the battlefield, and by the time they show up there's no need to lift a finger. The enemy has already been handled, and what triggered the movement of God was their commitment to praise and worship even in the face of doom.

What if we believed that this still happens today? That when I give God my praise and worship, this could be used to shift the atmosphere? What if we really believe God still chooses to move? That he will fight for me when I praise him, even when I may not feel like it?

If Michael Jackson can transform a television station from rock and roll to *Pimp My Ride*, how much more will the God of the universe respond to our praise by dismantling the principalities and powers that are positioned against us?

THE BLACK BABE RUTH?

But God chose what is foolish in the world to shame the wise;
God chose what is weak in the world to shame the strong.

1 Corinthians 1:27

American history often gets things backwards. Nowhere is this clearer than in the case of Josh Gibson (1911–1947), known for years as "The Black Babe Ruth"—a nickname Josh should have been offended by.

Gibson hit somewhere between eight hundred to a thousand career home runs. Ruth hit seven hundred and fourteen. Josh Gibson boasted a lifetime batting average almost twenty points higher than the Babe. The most home runs Babe Ruth hit in a season was sixty. Josh maxed out with sixty-nine. And Josh compiled his statistics while playing the last four years of his life with a brain tumor, which led to his untimely death at age thirty-five.[1] Babe retired at forty.

Josh never got a shot to play in the major leagues because of the "gentlemen's agreement" that banned him and his fellow black ballplayers. Eventually, Josh would get his due, though he never lived to see it. In 1972, Josh became one of the first players from the Negro Leagues to be inducted into the Major League Baseball hall of fame. And in 2024, Major League Baseball incorporated Negro League statistics, making Josh Gibson the all-time leader in batting average and slugging percentage (among other categories).

Most people still have never heard of him, because Josh Gibson is a reminder that to be black and great in America often comes with an asterisk. People wrongly assume that Josh played against inferior talent, which is why they saw his astronomical numbers as being inflated. In their eyes, Josh and the whole system he played in are second class, glorified minor leagues, weak.

"Weak." Now, that's a word Paul uses to describe how the Corinthians viewed him. Like any city steeped in first-century Greek culture, the Corinthians were obsessed with those who possessed extraordinary gifts of speech. You know the type: those who can move a crowd from laughter to tears with the flip of a phrase or the telling of a story. And then came Paul, who didn't rely on powers of Greek rhetoric, but on a man who, he said, had died on a cross and risen from the grave for the forgiveness of their sins. Paul was so convinced by the message of the cross that he intentionally stayed away from catchy phrases or moving stories. He didn't want their faith to rest in the messenger but in the message. Most in Corinth rejected that message, and even people in the church considered Paul to be in the minor leagues of speakers—boring and weak.

Now as one who makes his living with words, I can tell you nothing would keep me up at night more than the ridicule Paul experienced at the hands of the Corinthians. Do you know how many times I've berated myself over the mediocre (or downright bad) sermon I preached? How often I thought the story I told wasn't a good one, or how the joke didn't resonate, or how no one responded? It's unthinkable to me that what I flog myself over, Paul boasts in.

Why? Because Paul, in the context of talking about the power of the gospel versus the slickness of the messenger, says, "But God chose what is weak in the world to shame the strong" (1 Corinthians 1:27). God delights in taking what the world would put an asterisk next to and using it to make emphatic statements and unbreakable records. Why? So that he, and no one else, would get the glory.

Feeling weak? Feeling a touch like Josh Gibson, in that you've accomplished so much and gone unnoticed all at once? Don't think you've received your just due? Yeah, there's a place for standing up for yourself, but while you are in pursuit of justice, remember that God sees. And when we are weak, he has us just where he wants us. In our weakness, he is made strong.

It's been said that white fans who saw Josh Gibson, the "black Babe Ruth," play were so impressed that they started calling Babe Ruth the "white Josh Gibson." Going by the numbers, they're on to something.

HIGHWAY DIGNITY

Thy word is a lamp unto my feet, and a light unto my path.

Psalm 119:105 (KJV)

The highlight of my childhood summers was piling into our car and making the trip from Atlanta to Roanoke, Virginia to visit my grandparents. I can still smell my Nana's grits and fried apples. I loved sitting out on the old porch, listening to my grandfather tell stories of his brief baseball career and what life was like during Jim Crow. After about a week or so it would be time to leave, and Nana always packed us a lunch of fried chicken, boiled eggs, rice, and dessert. We'd say our goodbyes, pile back into the car, and pull out of the driveway to begin the journey back.

"Hey, Dad," one of us kids would say. "Why does Nana pack us a lunch? Doesn't she know there's places like McDonald's where we stop to eat?"

We kids would soon find out Nana was just doing what she'd always done, starting long before there were McDonald's or desegregated restaurants.

Imagine it's the height of Jim Crow and it's time for the annual road trip down south to visit your relatives. You're excited and apprehensive all at once. What happens if the car breaks down somewhere in Mississippi? How will your kids react when you're denied service at the restaurant? And what do you do when you're bone-tired in need of a good night's rest but that hotel tells you no because you are black?

Thanks to Victor Hugo Green (1892–1960), *The Negro Motorist Green Book*, published annually from 1936 to 1966, gave you the chance to avoid these inhumanities. Victor carefully laid out places where you could eat and get a good night's rest without being turned away or treated as less-than. What he offered was a generous portion of human self-worth, and black people came back for seconds. Walk into just about any black home during the time his book was published, and there it rests on the coffee table, igniting reminiscences and sparking community. The Green Book created an alternate universe among my tribe, allowing us to travel with our heads held high.

While the system of Jim Crow has ended, the road of life still has its share of potholes, slights, and troubles. *How do I know I can really trust those people? Am I supposed to say yes to that job on the other side of the country? How am I supposed to manage my money, or respond to that unkind person?*

The psalmist is like Victor Hugo Green when he writes, "Thy word is a lamp unto my feet, and a light unto my path" (Psalm 119:105 KJV). In the culture of his time, there were no streetlights; travel proved even more uncertain and dangerous than in Victor's day. To navigate the darkness, they would take lamps with them and hold them out just in front of their eyes—or even tie them to their ankles. What the lamp was to the ancient traveler, the psalmist says the Word of God is to us at all times.

You may have many questions: "How am I supposed to steward money?" "What do I look for in a potential spouse?" "What am I supposed to do with my life?" God has provided us with the original Green Book. His Word gives us guidance in discerning the answers to these questions and so much more.

It really was unthinkable for a person of color to venture down south on some road trip without taking Victor's book. In the same way, it should be beyond comprehension for us to navigate all of what life throws at us without consulting God's Book. In that book is everything we need.

MARVIN'S QUESTION

When the house of David was told, "Syria is in league with Ephraim," the heart of Ahaz and the heart of the people shook as the trees of the forest shake before the wind. . . .

Therefore the Lord himself will give you a sign. Behold the virgin shall conceive and bear a son, and shall call his name Immanuel.

Isaiah 7:2,14

On the third Friday in May of 1971, Motown's subsidiary Tamla released Marvin Gaye's album *What's Going On*. It would go on to make number one on *Rolling Stone*'s top five hundred albums of all time. And to think Marvin's masterpiece almost never saw the light of day.

It wasn't that Motown executives were a poor judge of talent. It's just that . . . that, what Marvin wanted to do was so off brand. Talk about a departure from such feel-good Motown songs like "My Girl" by the Temptations, or how the Supremes reminded us "You Can't Hurry Love." Or a little Stevie Wonder on his harmonica as we followed his instructions to "Say Yeah." *That* was Motown, not this. I mean, come on, have you listened to *What's Going On*? Marvin's singing about the war in Vietnam, protests, police brutality, and the senseless slaughter of blacks. Not a proven formula for stellar album sales. Marvin was messing with Barry Gordy's bottom line. But something in the record label's founder told him to try it.

Good call, Mr. Gordy.

What's Going On is timeless because injustice is. Put the album on, close your eyes, and it feels like you're on the streets of Minneapolis in the spring of 2020, or glued to your device on January 6th, 2021. Marvin's question continues to reverberate as wars, guns, racial violence, and injustice continue to have their way.

Smokey Robinson called Marvin's album prophecy. I wish he wasn't right. I'm ready for the question to stop being asked. Like, forever.

Forever will come, and for that I'm thankful. What Smokey called Marvin's album is what we should call Isaiah 7. The people of God have just gotten some disheartening news. An overwhelming army made up of several nations is coming for them. In descriptive language, we are told their response: their hearts "shook as the trees of the forest shake before the wind" (Isaiah 7:2).

Ever felt that way? Ever gotten a piece of news so bad you literally had to sit down to absorb it? Sure you have. When my wife and I found out our eight-year-old son had a rare blood disease and needed to spend time at St. Jude Children's Hospital, we "shook as trees." We were a cocktail of shock, sadness, and anger. I was beside myself with what, at times, felt like rage. Eight-year-olds aren't supposed to have their life flash before their eyes. Over the months to come, my prayers could be whittled down to three words—what's going on?

Ever been there? I'm guessing you have. Life has its shaking moments. As my grandmother used to say, if you haven't gone through something, keep living and you will. For all of us there are stretches of life's highway riddled with signage of one question, over and over and over again: "What's going on?"

In the middle of the Israelites' distress, God shows up. He tells them that help is on the way—in the form of a child who will be conceived by a virgin. Most comforting of all is the child's name Immanuel, which means "God is with us." Even if you're not very religious, you probably know the Christmas story: Mary, the mother of Jesus, was a virgin when she conceived Jesus. In Isaiah, God is giving the Israelites a prophecy of the coming of his Son. And when he comes, he will be with us.

Followers of Jesus aren't bubble wrapped from trouble. I wish it were the case, but it's just not true. We go through things. Very hard things. We all spend tours of duty in hospitals, the gravesites of loved ones, unjust firings, and the like. These moments bring to mind Marvin's question. But to every cry of "What's going on?" there's the answer of Immanuel, who grants comfort in his name. He gently reminds us of his presence. He whispers, "I am with you."

My son's first day at St. Jude's Children's Hospital did not get off to a good start. He had to get his blood taken, and he was not having it. He was screaming and the nurse could not get him to sit still long enough for her to take his blood. I stepped in, picked him up, and put him on my lap. I asked the nurse if she wouldn't mind taking my blood. She agreed.

As she grabbed my arm to get ready to draw blood, I asked Myles to watch Daddy, while I thought to myself, "You better not flinch!" The nurse found the vein and pressed the needle into my arm. The vial filled with blood. Myles took it all in—watching me and the nurse and the blood. When she was done, I asked Myles if he could be strong like Daddy and have his blood taken. He nodded his tear-stained face and stuck out his arm.

What changed? He still had to go through something which, moments before, had paralyzed him with fear. The difference was that his daddy was with him and had gone through the same unpleasant process.

I don't want to make light of your trouble. I only want to point out you're not the only one to ask Marvin's question. Jesus asked it too on the cross, when he wanted to know why God had forsaken him (Matthew 27:46). It was there on the old rugged cross, where Jesus was history's ultimate victim of injustice, being executed for our sins, that he had his blood drawn. When we find ourselves shaking in life's season of trouble, we can look to him and find the strength to endure.

DON'T WASTE YOUR PAIN

For we do not have a high priest who is unable to sympathize with our weaknesses, but one who in every respect has been tempted as we are, yet without sin. Let us then with confidence draw near to the throne of grace, that we may receive mercy and find grace to help in time of need.

Hebrews 4:15-16

I've long been fascinated by comedians, drawn in by their contradictions. By all appearances they are the funniest people on the planet. On closer inspection, they are some of the most miserable, tormented souls you'll come across.

John Belushi died of a drug overdose. John Candy struggled with severe anxiety and depression, all while he kept us in stitches. Robin Williams died by suicide.

And then there's Richard Pryor (1940–2005). The comedian's comedian. If there were a Mount Rushmore of comics, he would surely be etched in granite. Born in Peoria, Illinois, Richard grew up in a brothel run by his grandmother. His earliest memories were peering through a peephole, watching his mother turn tricks for customers. Richard's vision of manhood was far from ideal; he saw men of all colors wander in and shuffle out of his home of ill repute. As a teenager he was raped by another man.

Years later he would turn stages into therapy sessions, grasping for ways to make sense of it all. And here we thought he was just making things up to keep us doubled over in laughter. But there's Richard, a household name, flush with movie credits, album sales, and cash, while his childhood trauma would not let him go. He needed an outlet to process all of what he had gone through, so he reached for microphones, drugs, and women. He held on to the first two, but couldn't keep the last.

Somehow, Richard was able to package his pain and turn it into five Grammys, one Emmy, and a production company he launched with the aim of helping more people of color.

Don't take what I'm about to say as gospel truth, but more like an educated guess. Comedians are hailed for their brilliance, and rightly so, as they stand and keep people laughing for an hour. But I don't think their brilliance is found in the material they put together. Their real genius is when they decide to harvest all of the cruel things done to them and repurpose it for our pleasure. Great comics are keen observers, and the first thing they observe is what has happened to them. They figure out how to put it to good use.

Great comics don't waste their pain.

Neither did Jesus.

When we come to the book of Hebrews, we find a group of people who have experienced their own trauma. Since following Jesus, many had their property taken, others were thrown in jail, and still others were beaten. Unable to make sense of it all, they were on the edge of giving Jesus the peace sign and going back to navigating life on their own terms. In chapter four, the writer calls a time-out to remind them they aren't the only ones to go through pain. Jesus, the writer says, has gone through his own bit of trauma. He's on the other side and can sympathize with anything you may be going through. Because of this, the writer argues, you are not to withdraw from Jesus, but run to him.

I'm not sure how to say this, because it sounds so wrong. But if I'm tracking with the writer of Hebrews, he is saying that Jesus, *after* coming to earth, living among us, and suffering and dying for us, is now able to relate to us in ways he could not have before. Don't misunderstand me or the writer. Jesus was always enough. But let's see a universal principle of the human experience: handle pain right and it makes us better. One of the benefits is empathy.

Our Savior can now relate to our pain in much more real and empathetic ways because he had experienced pain and cruelty and injustice when he took on flesh and lived among us. He can empathize with our brokenness because he lived firsthand in a broken world. Jesus did not waste his pain. He is now able to see you in your struggles, nod his head, and connect.

And I also believe Jesus looked at Richard smoking crack cocaine not with condemnation but with tears and empathy, because he could relate to the brokenness of humanity. While I'm thankful Richard went to the stage to work out his pain, I can only hope he took a few more steps to go to the Savior. If he did so he would have met an empathetic Jesus.

I don't know what you see when, at the depths of your pain, you close your eyes and see Jesus. But if it's anything less than a vision of empathy, you've got the wrong picture.

It's been said that every time a man goes to a brothel he's looking for God.[1] That's because the men Richard saw growing up were themselves looking for a place to deal with their pain. That's all of us, isn't it? You may not go to a house of ill repute, but you may turn on the hookup app. Your medication may not be a stage, but it could be a store. Those things, and more, will never give you the healing you need. Only an empathetic Savior will.

21

OBAMA'S CROWN

For to this you have been called, because Christ also suffered for you, leaving you an example, so that you might follow in his steps.

1 Peter 2:21

On May 8, 2009, a little boy named Jacob Philadelphia stepped into the Oval Office. No, he wasn't there with some big tour, the kind that grants kids the privilege of taking in the sights of America's most famous home. Jacob was there because his father, Carlton Philadelphia, a staff member with the National Security Council, had called in some favors and wanted to give his child a picture of what could be. Jacob was just five when he walked into the room where it happens.

Looking back, Jacob would reflect on how big the Oval Office felt in his five-year-old mind, but the sensation of being overwhelmed didn't last long. He was distracted by the president. There was just something about him Jacob had to know.

What was it? Did it have to do with how President Barack Obama (1961–) was going to drag us out of the economic crisis he inherited?

Did Jacob want to find Sasha and Malia, the President's young daughters, so he could play with them?

Or was Jacob hungry, and needed to see if President Obama had any snacks in this great big office of his?

No, no, and no.

Jacob blurted out his question, but President Obama didn't understand. So Jacob said it a little louder. This time the leader of the free world got it, bent his head, and told Jacob, "Touch it, dude." As Jacob Philadelphia reached for the crown of President Obama's head, Pete Souza snapped one of the most iconic photographs in presidential history.

All this sweet black boy wanted to know was if President Barack Obama's hair was like his.

The photograph would come to embody the message President Obama campaigned on and wrote about—the audacity of hope and change. The moment would inspire something within Jacob as well. Over a decade later, fresh out of high school, Jacob Philadelphia would say of his meeting with the President: "That was a pretty big highlight of my life. . . . If I get to see another Black man be at the top, be at that pinnacle, then I want to follow that lead."[1]

The fires of inspiration within Jacob, sparked that day in the Oval Office, show no signs of dying out. He plans to attend the University of Memphis and study political science in the hopes of becoming president one day.

All from the touch of a crown of a man's head whose hair felt like his own.

We all are desperate for examples. It's why young girls are in a hurry to wear makeup like their mom, or boys to dress like their fathers. It's why fatherless boys are drawn to gangs, or kids who nurture dreams of playing in the pros hang posters of their favorite athletes on their bedroom walls. And it's why when a pastor fails, so many leave the church and even religion. Examples are powerful.

Peter understood this, which is why he calls Jesus our *example* (1 Peter 2:21). He's writing in Greek, and the Greek word for *example* is a compound word which means "under-writer." Remember when we were kids and we would trace images? We'd take something someone else had drawn and put a blank piece of paper on top of it, tracing the image onto that blank page. That's the idea behind the word *example*. Christ is the drawing, and we are the blank pages called to copy him onto our lives.

In his own way, Jesus is presenting himself as a model for us to emulate.

Or if I could say it in a more Oval-Officey way: Jesus is holding out his life and calling us to "Touch it, dude."

I'm horrible at drawing, but I'm world class at tracing. Like, world class! And here's the groundbreaking insight I've learned about tracing—and it's so worth the price you paid for this book—you can't be distracted and trace well. All you need to be an accomplished tracer like myself is focus. But isn't that the problem in our relationship with Christ? It's so easy to get distracted, to look away from his image and get caught up trying to trace other images in places like social media, the wrong kind of friends, or whatever the world has told us will lead us to the good life.

So what's distracting you? What has your attention more than Jesus? What's keeping you from reaching for the crown of Messiah Jesus?

22

90 SECONDS TO CAMELOT

But, knowing their hypocrisy, he said to them, "Why put me to the test? Bring me a denarius and let me look at it." And they brought one. And he said to them, "Whose likeness and inscription is this?" They said to him, "Caesar's." Jesus said to them, "Render to Caesar the things that are Caesar's, and to God the things that are God's." And they marveled at him.

Mark 12:15-17

Get your phone out. Go to your stopwatch. Ready? When I say, "Go," start the clock, begin reading, and keep going until I tell you to stop.

Go!

On the morning of October 25, 1960, Dr. Martin Luther King Jr. was taken to the Reidsville Penitentiary, two hundred miles from his home in Atlanta. Nothing new here, right? King going to jail is like any day of the week ending in *y*—common. But Reidsville was a different animal altogether, with a peculiar reputation for being rough on inmates. King's pregnant wife, Coretta, had every reason to be concerned for his life.

While King sat in his cell, Richard Nixon and John F. Kennedy were running step-for-step in the closest presidential race in US history. When news of King's predicament reached both candidates, Nixon decided to blow him off, assuming the black vote wasn't critical. Kennedy chose another path. He picked up the phone and placed a call to the frantic Coretta King.

He didn't say much, just a few words of compassion and the offer that if she needed him, he would be there. When Coretta hung up, she passed word of Kennedy's thoughtful gesture on to her father-in-law, who happened to be one of the most powerful and prominent pastors in America. Reverend Martin Luther King Sr. led a not-so-quiet campaign for Kennedy, along with the black press. He let it be known he was switching his party loyalties from Republican to Democrat and begged others to join him.[1]

Did his efforts work? I'll let you decide. Kennedy would win by around a measly hundred thousand votes. Just the previous election, in 1956, the Republican incumbent, President Eisenhower, had carried about sixty percent of the black vote. Now, in 1960, Democratic Kennedy would win with seventy percent of the black vote. Without that phone call to a distressed Mrs. King, Kennedy would not be president. How long did the call last? Ninety seconds. Maybe. Ninety seconds to—as the Kennedy years in the White House have been dubbed—"Camelot."

Ninety seconds that swung a generation of blacks to vote Democrat.

Ninety seconds, and blacks are still primarily voting Democrat.

What swung a whole group of people over wasn't a political platform, a fancy speech, or slick promises. What hooked African Americans was good old-fashioned empathy. (Or, at least, the appearance of empathy. I am not so naïve as to think that Kennedy didn't have an agenda.)

You can stop the clock now.

About the time it took to read this bit of history is about the length of Kennedy's call, and that call continues to have its hold on so many African Americans decades later.

I don't know what you're feeling with all of this political talk about Democrats and Republicans. Bothered? Triggered? Squeamish? And here I am not just talking politics but doing so in the context of race! Boy, am I asking for it.

Jesus found himself cornered one day. He was asked a very political question about whether one should pay taxes to Caesar. Mark makes it clear these two groups who confronted Jesus were not there out of curiosity; they had an agenda, "to trap him in his talk" (Mark 12:13). On one side, meet the Herodians, a group of people who were devoted to the Jewish King Herod; Herod had been allowed a measure of power to rule under the Roman regime. Clearly, they were in favor of paying taxes to Caesar, who afforded them their power. They knew where their bread was buttered. On the other side were the Pharisees. They were anti-Rome. In their mind, no Messiah of theirs would dare think of paying taxes to Caesar, because he would come to overthrow Rome and set up his own earthly kingdom.

Jesus was in a no-win situation. Or so it seemed.

Cornered, Jesus asked for a coin—and then asked them a question. He wanted to know whose image was on the coin. They answered, of course, that it was Caesar's. Jesus shrugged his shoulders and said his version of, "Okay, give it to him. Pay your taxes." I can imagine the Herodians were smiling and the Pharisees were seething.

"Oh, one more thing," Jesus says. "Since we are going to give Caesar what belongs to him, don't forget to give God what belongs to him."

The scene ends with both Herodians and Pharisees marveling at Jesus. Huh?

The key word here is *likeness*, or *image*. Since the coin has Caesar's image on it, give it to him. But since we have been made in the image of God, bearing his likeness on our lives, let's give *ourselves* to God. Jesus is saying that while the coin belongs to Caesar, your life belongs to God. The mark someone bears tells you who they belong to. Or to say it another way, image is ownership.

Government gets the coin. God gets your life.

That's good to remember going into any election cycle, where tensions run high and we look down on the other side as we think our share of how-could-yous when it comes to who they are voting for. Don't get me wrong. Christians should be involved in the political process and be passionate about issues the Bible speaks clearly about. Let's not forget, Jesus does not avoid the subject of paying taxes. He just refuses to put his ultimate sense of hope on a political issue. Caesar is only entitled to a fraction of our money. God is entitled to all of our lives.

And let's also not miss the lesson of empathy in Kennedy's call. People are not so much moved by ideological positions and arguments as much as they are by relationship and empathy—two things missing from our political discourse. When you find things getting a little heated, why don't you step away from the keyboard? Put down your clever argument and pick up the phone for a chat. You probably won't need more than ninety seconds.

A WARM PRESENCE

Soon afterward he went on through cities and villages, proclaiming and bringing the good news of the kingdom of God. And the twelve were with him, and also some women who had been healed of evil spirits and infirmities: Mary, called Magdalene, from whom seven demons had gone out, and Joanna, the wife of Chuza, Herod's household manager, and Susanna, and many others, who provided for them out of their means.

LUKE 8:1-3

Outside of a few scant details, we don't know much about Alice H. Parker. She was born in 1895, but we have no clue when she died. We don't know what she looks like. Google her, and a picture of an unrelated white woman by the same name comes up. She graduated from Howard University. We think she was a cook who married a butler.[1] And she had to have been a woman of little patience who didn't take no for an answer. After all, what black woman files a United States patent on December 23, 1919, two days before Christmas, six months after women got the right to vote, and decades before Jim Crow would end? Do you know how difficult it is to file a patent? But when you live in New Jersey, and your home is cold, and you are an educated person, you tend to figure it out.[2]

We may not know what Alice looked like, when she died, or many other details of her life, but what we do know is that her patent laid the groundwork for the modern-day heating system in our homes. Yep, next time the temperature drops and you go to your thermostat, you have a black woman to thank.

We may not see her, but boy, do we feel her.

Have you ever wondered how Jesus' ministry was able to exist? I mean they had to eat, buy clothes, pay the customary tax on travel and goods, and cover a host of other expenses. And Jesus couldn't look to his followers for financial support. After all, Peter, James, and other disciples had left their jobs to follow him. Yeah, Jesus could have performed miracles to pay their expenses (which he did on one occasion in Matthew 17:24-27), but he chose not to. Instead, he turned his attention to the most unlikely people in that culture for help: a group of women. Let's read Luke 8:1-3 and consider the women who supported Jesus' ministry.

Now, I wish I could tell you all about these women, pointing out all the interesting details and facts about their lives. I'd love to blow your mind with their stories. But truthfully, we just don't know much about them, and I think this is where the beauty lies. See, these women played an essential role in the life and ministry of Jesus and his disciples. They funded the ministry that started the church, offered salvation to the world, and changed millions—if not billions—of lives. Contrary to what we may see on social media, these women show you don't have to have a large following to be an influencer. They teach us that popularity and importance are not the same. Like Alice, we may not know much about them, but believe me, their presence was felt.

I need to hear this word, and maybe you do too. Ours is a culture filled with people frantic to be known, to build a reputation based on what they've accomplished. But if I understand Alice Parker right—and, even more so, the women who funded Jesus—what really matters is being a part of something greater than yourself. It's what drove Alice to go through the arduous process of filing a patent, and what moved women like Joanna to Cash App Jesus. We were created for far more than to be the documentarians of our own lives. It's when we stitch the narrative of ourselves to something and Someone greater that true influence happens. You don't have to be seen to be felt.

But there's more. I don't know about you, but I find it easy to name-drop or buddy up to the people who society esteems. It's easy to be fluent in name-dropping, but this is not the way of Jesus. He chose to live in proximity with people who were unknown and easily looked over.

Of course, Jesus also made room for the well-known and important. But I've found it's good for my soul to make room for the Alice Parkers and Joannas of our world. There's just something about doing life with people whose value can't be verified by a blue check or quantified by the amount of likes, clicks, or followers they have accrued.

I GOTTA BE ME

The Samaritan woman said to him, "How is it that you, a Jew, ask for a drink from me, a woman of Samaria?" (For Jews have no dealings with Samaritans.)

John 4:9

What does it mean to act black?

If I use slang, does that make me black? Or if I use words like *coalesce* and *genuflect*, do I now have to turn in my African American Express card? What does it mean to act black?

No, really, I'd like to know. Because when I made good grades in high school, I was told I needed to stop "acting white." I made it a point not to let people know my test scores from then on.

Am I more black if I marry a black woman, or less black if I don't?

If I become a Q and throw up the hooks, does that make me black? Or if I have no idea what the previous sentence means, does it make me less black? Please tell me, what does it really mean to act black?

Sammy Davis Jr. (1925–1990) gives us no help to our question; he only complicates the matter. He was born and came of age in the black Mecca of Harlem, yet he allowed himself to be the butt of racist jokes on some of the world's biggest stages by his white "Rat Pack" friends. He fell in love with a white actress, was told to cut it off, marry a black woman or he'd be dead. So he did, paying the black woman a sum of money for the sham wedding. A few years later he married a white woman, divorced her, then married a black woman—for real this time. He was a black Jew who spoke Yiddish and prayed at the Wailing Wall.

Sammy was friends with John F. Kennedy until the new president refused to let him come to his inauguration ball because of Sammy's then-white wife. So Sammy Davis Jr. would turn around and endorse a known racist whose policies were widely regarded as being harmful to the black community—Richard Nixon—all while becoming one of the biggest financial donors to the civil rights movement.

I'm so confused right now. It gets worse . . .

On August 22, 1972, at the Republican National Convention in Miami, Florida, Sammy Davis Jr. got on stage and hugged Richard Nixon. It was the worst photo op of his life. In the weeks and months following the hug seen round the world, his office was flooded with hate mail. So vile was the mail, his own secretary refused to let him see it. Sammy's invitations began to dry up, and understandably so. It would be sort of like Kendrick Lamar kibitzing with Trump. Not the greatest career move one could make.

To so many, Sammy had officially lost his black card.

With his career in jeopardy, Sammy reached out to Jesse Jackson and invited himself to Jesse's "Save the Children" event in the heart of Chicago. The lineup was stocked with black celebrities, and the theater was crammed with black people. If Sammy was going to resurrect from the beating he had taken, he had about three minutes to do it. So he walked out on stage and said: "I am here because I have come home as a black man. Disagree if you will with my politics, but I will not allow anyone to take away the fact that I am black."[1]

The audience erupted in applause. Did I mention they were black?

And what did he sing? His classic, of course: "I Gotta Be Me."

That moment when Sammy Davis Jr. gave Nixon a hug? Picture that when Jesus and his disciples walked into Samaria in John chapter four. No self-respecting Jew would ever go to or through Samaria. You went *around* Samaria. You didn't stop there, and if you did, you would have been less than Jewish—a real Sammy Davis Jr. But not Jesus. He stops, sends his disciples to the grocery store for some lunch, and strikes up a conversation with a Samaritan woman. Chances are no other Jews were there to see this. If they had, they would have been as disgusted as most black people in 1972 who saw Sammy embrace and endorse Nixon.

Not long into the conversation the Samaritan woman says something interesting to Jesus: "How is it that you, a Jew, ask for a drink from me, a woman of Samaria?" (John 4:9). I say this is interesting because Jesus did not introduce himself as a Jew. He didn't say one word about his ethnicity or culture. So how would she know unless

Jesus looked Jewish, dressed Jewish, spoke like a Jew, and had mannerisms like one? I guess what John is pointing out is that Jesus—God in the flesh—did not distance himself from his embodied reality. He came as a Jew.

But on the other hand, the woman is confused because even though Jesus presents as a Jew, he's doing some very un-Jewish things—like stopping in Samaria and engaging a Samaritan woman in conversation at a well in the middle of the day. He looks Jewish, but he for sure ain't acting Jewish. Why is Jesus transgressing the cultural norms of his people? Because of the greater purpose of the gospel. His whole reason for coming to Samaria was to take the good news to an ethnically different people.

This is the tension every Christ-follower should feel. On the one hand, we are embodied beings made in the image of God; we should joyfully celebrate our ethnicity and culture. On the other hand, our ultimate identity should be placed in the God who sent his Son to die for us and who has saved us. When we do this, we will at times transgress cultural boundaries, leaving us vulnerable to critiques of cultural compromise and being less than what is expected of us. But unlike Sammy, we are not working for the approval of our ethnic kin, but for the applause of God. If we are not under fire at times for being seen as compromising cultural assumptions and narratives, maybe the gospel isn't our bottom line.

Oh, the pain Sammy must have felt in the months after his infamous hug. Those who castigated him as an Uncle Tom cannot have known the extraordinary number of people Sammy bailed out of jail during the civil rights movement. Few gave more money to the cause of justice than Sammy, and now here he was, having to perform for his black card.

Jesus knew the pain as well. He came unto his own, and his own did not receive him (John 1:11). Like Sammy, Jesus refused to compromise what he believed. Instead, he got on the cross and stood on the world's stage, offering his life as a ransom for the world.

JOE LOUIS . . . THE GOLFER?

Then Mordecai told them to reply to Esther, "Do not think to yourself that in the king's palace you will escape any more than all the other Jews. For if you keep silent at this time, relief and deliverance will rise for the Jews from another place, but you and your father's house will perish. And who knows whether you have not come to the kingdom for such a time as this?"

Esther 4:13-14

In 1938, the boxer Joe Louis (1914–1981) beat the German Max Schmeling in a sold-out Yankee Stadium. His victory over Schmeling renewed American hope and pride as the Nazi regime was beginning to gain traction. Having barely broken a sweat after his first-round victory, Joe Louis was the toast of the town . . . shoot, the toast of the country.

In a sense, Joe Louis was groomed for this. His black boxing champion predecessor, Jack Johnson, had been way too much of an individual. Jack loved to flaunt his white women and talk trash to his white opponents as he toyed with and then pummeled them in the ring. And he did all of this right around the same time the Titanic was sinking. (By the way, Jack Johnson tried to get a first-class ticket to board the ship but was turned down because of his race.) Jack so ticked off the white establishment that they came up with a law to throw him in jail.

And then came Joe Louis.

Determined to prevent Joe from mimicking Johnson's rebellion, his handlers told him to never be photographed by himself with a white woman. To always smile and never talk trash. Joe needed to be respectful and not ruffle feathers or make white people uncomfortable in the least. He abided by these rules . . . for a while.

In 1935, the black heavyweight champion, Joe Louis, picked up the game of golf at the historic Langston Hughes Golf Course—one of the first courses built exclusively for African Americans. Joe became so good at the game (he was a two handicap) that a year after retirement he was invited to play in the San Diego Open, which is interesting because the people who extended the invitation forgot to read the PGA Tour bylaws—which permitted "Caucasian Only" professionals. No problem, Louis reasoned; he wasn't a professional. Problem solved. Louis teed it up and played the first two rounds, but missed the cut, all while making history as the first non-Caucasian to compete in a PGA Tour event.

With his brief two-round stint on the tour over, Louis was just getting started in his efforts to integrate the PGA. His days of flashing his teeth for the camera and playing nice were done. He leveraged every ounce of influence, and took every opportunity he could to bang on the door of the PGA to let non-whites in. And it paid off. Nine years after his San Diego debut, the black golfer Charlie Sifford would get his PGA Tour card. Six years later, Charlie would become the first minority golfer to win a PGA event.

As a young golfer, Tiger Woods drew inspiration from Sifford, even naming his son after Charlie. And when Tiger got his opportunity to host his own PGA event, he chose to give a tournament exemption to a minority player named Marcus Byrd. And where did Marcus grow up playing the game of golf? You guessed it, the Langston Hughes Golf Course—the same one where Joe Louis learned and fell in love with the game.

Joe Louis to Charlie Sifford to Tiger Woods and beyond . . .

Sometimes you've got to say something to start something.

Closed mouths really don't get fed. This is Mordecai's message to the newly crowned Jewish queen Esther. A sinister plot has just been discovered that would extinguish the Jewish people—unless someone intervenes. Queen Esther is the obvious person to stop the murders before they happen. She's a Jew. She occupies a position of power with great influence. But there's also risk involved. If she says something, she could lose her position, if not her life. Mordecai reminds her that the seat she sits on was not just for her to take a bunch of pictures and be adored by the masses. In the scheme of things, she was in her place for a far greater purpose. As Mordecai famously says, Esther has been raised up "for such a time as this" (Esther 4:14).

You're probably not a king or a queen, but you do have a measure of influence. It may be at your job, your school, your church, or with your kids. We all have been given some influence, and, like money, it needs to be stewarded well for the benefit of others. Esther, at great risk to herself, opened up her mouth, and the Jews were spared. Joe Louis stopped smiling, made some withdrawals from his influence account, and used it to open doors previously shut to minorities. And in the ultimate example, Jesus stepped out of the comforts of heaven and used his divine privilege to set us free.

All of us have been given a measure of influence. For some, it's the privilege of growing up in a two-parent home. For others, it's a college or postgraduate degree. For still others, it's a powerful position at your job. All of us have learned a lot from the great and poor decisions we have made. No matter how much or little is placed in your hand, there's someone out there who could benefit from what you have, the seat you occupy, or the lessons you have learned. So the next time you go to your work, school, or church, consider: "I've been sent here for such a time as this. How can I open doors for others?"

HOW LONG, O LORD?

How long, O Lord? Will you forget me forever?
How long will you hide your face from me?
How long must I take counsel in my soul
and have sorrow in my heart all the day?
How long shall my enemy be exalted over me?

Consider and answer me, O Lord my God;
light up my eyes, lest I sleep the sleep of death,
lest my enemy say, "I have prevailed over him,"
lest my foes rejoice because I am shaken.

But I have trusted in your steadfast love;
my heart shall rejoice in your salvation.
I will sing to the Lord,
because he has dealt bountifully with me.

Psalm 13

In the fall of 1932, advertisements appeared in Macon County, Alabama, inviting people to come in for free blood tests. Hundreds of poor black men signed up. While many were "diagnosed" with what was called "bad blood," what they didn't realize was that they were taking part in an official study known as the "Tuskegee Study of Untreated Syphilis in the Negro Male" run by the United States Public Health Service.

Of the six hundred men who would become a part of the study, three hundred and ninety-nine had already contracted the venereal disease, while the other two hundred and one were a part of the control group. None of them were treated. When a cure for syphilis was discovered in the 1940s, the American government refused to make it available to the men. They were simply curious to know how the disease would affect them over the course of their lives.

Curious.

The study ran for forty years, wreaking havoc on the men, their loved ones, and the broader community. Some of their wives contracted the disease. Many of their children were born with physical disabilities directly related to syphilis. Some of the men became blind. Others lost their minds—literally. Many died because of the disease. All under the gaze of a watching government who hid the cure in one hand and took notes on their suffering with the other.

Finally, in 1973, the United States settled with these men and their descendants for ten million dollars.

Let's do a little math, and we won't account for taxes or legal fees. (I understand it was originally 399 men with the disease, but, due to the government's neglect, many more contracted syphilis. The number of individuals who fell ill with syphilis despite the availability of a cure was certainly larger than 600 in the end, but we'll stick with that number to simplify things.) Ten million dollars divided by the 600 men who unknowingly took part in this study equals just over $16,000 per person.

Now let's say each man was married with two kids (a conservative estimate), so we will divide sixteen thousand by four, and give about four thousand dollars to each of these individuals. Take that number and divide it by the number of years the study ran, which is forty, and you have the annual price of a suffering black person: $100 a year. Did I say we won't count taxes or legal fees?

What's the going rate for a suffering black person? *One hundred dollars a year.*

These kinds of stories continue to weigh heavily on the black consciousness. It's no secret black people, and particularly black men, have a disproportionate fear of the medical industry. Among my own circle of friends, we constantly check in with each other to make sure we follow through on our annual physicals, get our colonoscopies, and take our medication. We need to be prodded because lurking beneath the surface is an assumption that we won't be properly cared for or something bad will be discovered, as if not going to the doctor would make the fear of what they may find disappear.

But the question of health is not the only one; so is the question of God. Where is he in the midst of such evil? It's one thing to make a poor choice and contract a venereal disease. It's quite another for someone to have the cure, not tell you about it, and watch you and your whole family suffer. It doesn't get more evil than that.

David, the author of Psalm 13, was not afraid to ask God's whereabouts as he navigated the valleys and dark places of life. Four times he asks a question which some of the Tuskegee Study men must have asked: "How long?" Here David is helping us to see that it's one thing to suffer, but quite another to not know how long we will suffer.

Then David ups the ante. He moves from his psychological torment to the spiritual agony of feeling as if God has abandoned him. That's *why* David wants to know how long God will hide his face from him. In the Bible, the face of God is the favor of God (Numbers 6:24-26). For God's face to be turned away is for God to have abandoned David in the suffering.

Ever felt as if God has abandoned you in the face of hardship?

And then David screams at God. The Hebrew words he writes for *consider* and *answer* are imperatives, which means they're commands. When a person makes a command, there's an emotional urgency attached. In other words, David is probably raising his voice at God, wanting answers about his suffering.

Ever been there? Ever pounded your fist, raised your voice, or cried tears of outrage at God over the injustice you have found yourself in?

If there was ever a psalm that resonated with the black experience in America, it's Psalm 13. Can't you hear the slaves asking "How long?" as they endured months at sea in the Middle Passage and hundreds of years in slavery? Can't you hear our ancestors demanding answers from God through the decades of Jim Crow? And can't you hear the cries of these Alabama men who needlessly suffered?

And then there's you and me. No, injustice does not discriminate. You could be Korean, Mexican, German, or another ethnicity, but keep living and hard times will knock on our door. You may have just discovered the affair. Someone may have stolen some money from you, or had a private meeting slandering you, which knocked you out of the running for a promotion. Or maybe you ask your own "How long?" as you deal with a loved one's addiction. What now?

We do what David does. And we do what black people have done for centuries. We drag ourselves, with all of our heartache and questions, to God.

Do you see how the Psalm ends? David pivots from wondering where God is to singing and rejoicing in his goodness—even though there's not a hint of resolution to his trauma or one answer to his questions. We call this faith. To sing and rejoice in a God you feel tormented by is an act of defiance to your circumstances. When you choose to keep showing up and singing and rejoicing in a God you *say* is good, even when you don't *feel* as if he is good, you are shaking your fist in the face of your situation. You are saying, "Not today. You will not rob me of my joy."

Our feelings are real and need to be acknowledged. But our feelings are like a two-year-old child. We put them in the car, strap them in, and interact with them. We do not put them in the trunk and ignore them. Nor do we give them the keys and put them behind the wheel.

Acknowledge your feelings. Bring them to God. Scream at God if you have to; he can handle it. But at the end of the day, give faith in God the keys, not feelings about God. Resolve to sing and rejoice even amidst the uncertainty. When we do, we announce to ourselves who our God is, and where in this world our hope truly resides.

EMMIT'S "SHOES"

And God saw everything that he had made, and behold, it was very good.

Genesis 1:31

Once, when Michael Jordan was nearing the end of his career with the Washington Wizards, a player on the opposing team decided to talk trash to MJ, accusing him of not being the player he once was. Michael flashed his trademark smile, pointed to his rival's feet, and said, "Yeah, but you're wearing my shoes."

That's kind of how I feel writing about Emmit McHenry (1943–) amidst all the online chatter about removing black history from so many schools. Don't these people understand every time they read an internet article campaigning against black history, or every time someone uses the medium to post something racially offensive, they are using a black man's invention?

Yep, every time you go online, surf the net, and send an email, you have Emmit McHenry to thank. He created a complex code which allowed any person the ability to search the internet and use email without having to be some computer genius. In other words, McHenry made the internet truly worldwide, accessible to anyone.

Whenever you check your bank account from your device, that's because of Emmit.

When you pay your bills online, that's Emmit again.

Doing research and need to run something by Google? There goes that man again.

Shoot, go to anywhere.com and there's Emmit McHenry lurking.

Where would we be without this black man?

Satisfaction doesn't even come close to what Emmit McHenry must feel. He has left his fingerprints in every corner of our world. There's something about the act of creating and cultivating in such a way in which the world is bettered that causes our souls to exhale. To create and enhance is to be like God. Can't you see the joy on God's face in the opening sentences of Genesis where every time he makes something he fist pumps and says, "Good!" No one, not even Emmit McHenry, had a more fulfilling week at work than God.

We were created to work, to enhance, to better. Work is not some curse God pronounced on Adam and Eve *after* they sinned. God was at work *before* they got here. And even before their sin, God called man and woman to work (Genesis 1:28). When we die and are taken up to the new heavens and new earth, work will be a part of our eternal reality (Isaiah 65:17-25). To labor is not a necessary evil we must put up with, but a part of God's good design for us. While there is some work which is destructive and evil (e.g., the selling of illegal substances or sex trafficking), to labor is a part of what it means to live in God's image. Everyone should be able to see their daily exertions as part of a broader narrative of God's redemptive will on this planet.

All of us should know a kind of satisfaction Emmit McHenry feels—the joy of knowing his work has caused a lot of good. (We would do well to note that many have taken his work and used it for bad, such as the online porn industry.)

But like everything else in life, there were some thorns attached to Emmit's invention. Because of McHenry's success, the United States government awarded his company a contract. The agreement was they would create and manage a registry of domains. The problem was, because his deal was with the government, he could not raise his contract fees. Under intense financial pressure, he sold his company for just under five million dollars in 1995.[1] Less than one year after the sale, the company that bought Emmit's would make twenty-one billion dollars off his work.

Was Emmit McHenry taken advantage of? Sure he was. But none of this negates the indelible mark he has left on our world. From the moment a child first figures out an iPad to the hospital staff who will care for them as they lie at death's door, Emmit's "shoes" have touched us all.

WHAT'S MY NAME?

The Son of Man came eating and drinking, and they say, "Look at him! A glutton and a drunkard, a friend of tax collectors and sinners!" Yet wisdom is justified by her deeds.

Matthew 11:19

In the leadup to their fight in the Houston Astrodome, Ernie Terrell refused to call Muhammad Ali (1942–2016) by his preferred Muslim name. Instead, he chose to call him by his birth name, Cassius Clay. Ernie should never—and I mean never—have done that. Ali was already on edge. He had refused to be inducted into the armed services to fight in Vietnam, and his options for staying out of prison were running out. And then Terrell decided to poke the bear. Bad call.

Ali responded by giving his usual pre-fight prophecy, but with an out-of-character nastiness. He told Terrell he was going to punish him, slapping him in their interview with the inimitable Howard Cosell. And then Ali bit his lip and called Terrell those words: "Uncle. Tom."

I honestly can't think of a more demeaning thing for one black person to call another. But it's especially unfortunate we use those words, because we've got our history completely screwed up on this one. If I had been at the press conference and could've read Ali's mind, I would have pulled his coattail and whispered in his ear, "Hey champ, don't do it. You're actually giving him the highest of compliments."

The epithet comes from the bestselling novel of the nineteenth century, *Uncle Tom's Cabin*, written by Harriet Beecher Stowe. The book was an immediate hit, selling around three thousand copies its first day. The demand would be so high, it took more than a dozen printers running around the clock just to keep up. The book would morph into a stage play, with white actors dressed up in blackface and using broken language, all while depicting Tom as a bumbling sellout to his race.

Nothing could be further from the truth.

By Harriet's own admission, the man she had in mind for Tom was Josiah Henson (1789–1883). Listen to what she says: "A last instance parallel with that of Uncle Tom is to be found in the published memoirs of the venerable Josiah Henson . . . now pastor of the missionary settlement at Dawn, in Canada."[1]

Did you catch that? Harriet had read the "published memoirs" of Josiah Henson's life, which helped her construct the character of Uncle Tom. What black man has a memoir of his life written in the nineteenth century? Must have been an important man who had accomplished a lot. Plus, she called him "venerable"—a word which means "to command respect." I can think of a lot of words to use for a person who is a sellout to their race, but "venerable" is not one of them.

Turns out Josiah was a slave who escaped to Canada. Not long into freedom, Josiah would risk his life by making several trips down south to rescue some 118 slaves, ushering them to a new life in Canada. Josiah was an entrepreneur who gave the newly emancipated slaves jobs. He was so successful as an entrepreneur that he won a medal at the first World's Fair in London. Josiah would finally spill his life as a slave, leader of the Underground Railroad, entrepreneur, and pastor onto paper in the form of a memoir, inspiring Harriet's character Uncle Tom. Today, Josiah's cabin is a small museum in his hometown of Dresden, Ontario, where some two hundred descendants of the slaves he freed resided.

All of this, and we come to the place where "Uncle Tom" means someone is a discredit to their race?

Who hasn't known the pain, anger, or frustration of being misunderstood, of having words said about them or assumptions made which were nowhere near the truth? I'm sure you've been down that street. I have. And so has Jesus. Can't you hear his exhaustion as he regurgitates what people have said about him? I mean, they called Jesus a "glutton and a drunkard" (Matthew 11:19). I don't know how they could have gotten this about the Messiah. Maybe things got lost in translation when word drifted from Cana about the miracle of water becoming wine. But Jesus, a drunkard? Jesus needing to sit in some recovery group because he just can't put the bottle down?

As far as we can tell, Jesus, in the words of my grandmother, didn't pay that no mind. He didn't spend his life obsessively checking social media or googling his name to see what people were saying about him. He didn't have some sort of neurotic compulsion to scan his list of followers constantly to see who dropped off or unfriended him. People are going to, well, *people*. We are not called to be the directors of our own PR firms.

As far as we can tell, Josiah didn't lose much sleep over how *Uncle Tom* was beginning to be portrayed in the broader culture. He knew who he was. He had set free over a hundred black people and employed them as well. He was spending his days preaching God's Word.

So what's got you bent out of shape? I'm not saying you shouldn't correct people when they've made wrongful assumptions about you. I am saying: keep things in perspective. Obsess over pleasing God, not people. Most times if you do the former, the latter will take care of itself. Concentrate on character, not reputation—who you really are, not who people think you are. You can never control reputation. You can control character.

29

WHITNEY'S WAY

First of all, then, I urge that supplications, prayers, intercessions, and thanksgivings be made for all people, for kings and all who are in high positions, that we may lead a peaceful and quiet life, godly and dignified in every way.

1 Timothy 2:1-2

Black people have always had a complicated relationship with the American flag. We went off to war and fought for the United States only to come back and be told to wait for our food in the back of the restaurant, which was standard for Jim Crow establishments of the time.

When Muhammad Ali was denied service at a restaurant because of the color of his skin, he took the new gold medal he had won in the 1960 Rome Olympics and hurled it into the Ohio River. Before the decade was out, he would be one of the most hated men in

America for his refusal to fight in the Vietnam War. But who could forget a trembling Ali, holding the Olympic torch in his hand before a watching world, dressed in the patriotic colors of his home country to announce the start of the 1996 Games? It just doesn't get more complicated than that.

And then there's Whitney Houston (1963–2012).

Before she stepped on to the field to sing the national anthem on January 27, 1991, she was little Ms. Compliant, nodding her head and doing everything she was told. The architects of her brand had carefully constructed an image of a colorless Whitney, who had gained so much crossover appeal you would never know she had grown up in the black church, was hood to the core, and carried on an intimate relationship with a woman. But at the close of her breakout decade, her proverbial slip was starting to show. She was booed by a black audience who deemed her a sellout at the 1989 Soul Train Awards. At the same ceremony, Whitney met Bobby Brown, the bad boy of R&B, and the two began a torrid romance—to the disappointment of her handlers.

The woman affectionately known as "The Voice" was starting to rebel.

With all of this lurking in the background, Whitney carried her quiet protest to the 1991 Super Bowl and readied herself to sing the national anthem. I don't know how many other candidates the powers that be considered, but it shouldn't have been more than one.

America was in the middle of the Gulf War, and the country was filled with uncertainty. When Whitney stepped onto the stage, I was in the final semester of my senior year in high school, just days away from turning eighteen. I had many conversations with my classmates wondering if there would be a draft. We didn't know. And we asked why we, as black men, would want to fight for a country that never seemed to have fought for us. But by the time Whitney was done singing "The Star-Spangled Banner," we would have taken a bullet for America. We were that moved.

Not long after she accepted the invitation, she confided in her music producer how much Marvin Gaye's interpretation of the national anthem at the 1983 NBA All-Star Game had inspired her.[1] However he arranged the anthem, she needed more space, more freedom to interject the subtle gospel riffs and runs which were a part of the real Whitney, the part she had stuffed for the past decade in an attempt to appease her representatives. But those days were fading. If she was going to sing it, it had to be done *her* way.

And so he added one extra beat per measure (which the orchestra hated), recorded the new arrangement, and sent it off to Whitney. She never listened to it until a few days before her performance. When she finally sat down to listen, Whitney closed her eyes and took it all in. When it was over, she whispered, "I got it," and went to record the anthem. (When she performed the anthem at the Super Bowl, Whitney sang into a dead microphone, and we heard her recorded version.) It only took one take, which is what the world heard that Super Bowl Sunday.

I don't know if you've ever really listened to the "Star-Spangled Banner," but it's a pretty violent song, with rockets and guns and war (not to mention slavery). But what Whitney used her extra measures to highlight was not blood and gore, but freedom and bravery—themes she was beginning to ache for in her own life. And when she was done you were either crying, ready to go off to war, or both. Post-anthem, no one picked up on her little rebellion. Some whites called her a good Christian woman, and her popularity went through the stratosphere. Next came *The Bodyguard* and her classic cover of "I Will Always Love You."

But Whitney couldn't keep up the charade. In a move which caused the world to scratch their heads, she married Bobby Brown, drifted off into drugs, went to rehab, and tragically died in the bathtub of the Beverly Hilton hotel of an apparent overdose. When her post-anthem career began to nosedive, people begged her to get back to her Ms. Compliant roots. She refused. I think she understood that America never really loved who she was—they loved who they thought she was.

Read the Bible and you'll see followers of Jesus are put in a real bind when it comes to the world. We are told that while we are in the world, we are not to be of the world (Romans 12:1-2). We are called to care for society, without falling in love with her. In one key story, we see Daniel working for corporate Babylon, allowing them to change his name to that of a pagan god (Daniel 1). But then he openly defies the king's edict by praying to his Lord (Daniel 6). Yes, God is to have our ultimate allegiance, but while we are praying to him, we need to include "kings and all who are in high positions" in our prayers (1 Timothy 2:2).

Think about the implications of praying for "all who are in high positions." Yes, that would include both Republicans and

Democrats. A conservative-leaning Supreme Court or one tilted toward the left.

Pray, Paul says, for all who are in high places.

You may not like the pilot of your airplane, but you would do well to pray for her. Her successes or failures will have a direct impact on your well-being. And so it is with our leaders.

It seems as if with each passing election cycle, things get more and more contentious in America. It's especially so with the church. I don't know what your prayers are like for our leaders, but it feels as if we don't have a real posture of prayer for those who are in authority. It's hard to be mean toward people you are earnestly praying for. What if we took Paul's instructions to heart? No, our political convictions may not change, but how we express them certainly would.

One more thing. Whitney's original plan was to sing the anthem in a black cocktail dress and heels, which would have been more than appropriate given the occasion. But at the last minute she decided to go with a tracksuit. Yep. She sang the most patriotic song *her* way. She not only crooned of freedom, she looked free. All while some seven hundred and fifty million people watched.

Just thirty-two days later, the Gulf War ended. I might be wrong, but I'd like to believe that Whitney's complicated interpretation of the anthem, with all of its freedom accents, inspired a sense of urgency among our troops to advance the cause of freedom for all people.

THE DEFIANT MARY LUMPKIN

And Jacob was left alone. And a man wrestled with him until the breaking of the day. When the man saw that he did not prevail against Jacob, he touched his hip socket, and Jacob's hip was put out of joint as he wrestled with him. Then he said, "Let me go, for the day has broken." But Jacob said, "I will not let you go unless you bless me."

Genesis 32:24-26

As the father of adult sons who have all moved out of the home (at least for the moment) I have been cursed with hindsight, and I can tell you that compliance is overrated. I know, there is something to be said for eating your dinner before dessert, being home by curfew, and always telling the truth. But where would the world be without an appropriate measure of rebellion?

Every invention came about through stubborn people who just wouldn't abide by the word "no." When Frederick Douglass was deemed to be uncontrollable by his master, he was sent to a man notorious for beating slaves into submission. It didn't work. Frederick fought for hours with his handler and won. Had Malcolm Little not pushed back against his boarding school authorities, allowed jail to break his spirit, or caved to the edict of the Honorable Elijah Muhammad demanding his silence, he just wouldn't be Malcolm X. And had John Lewis and his SNCC colleagues accepted their first assault and walked away in resignation, we would not have the legislative reforms and freedoms we enjoy today.

On the whole, black people have always been a rebellious lot, choosing the path of "good trouble" as we marched in defiance of unjust systems and laws. Who knows where we would be if we played the part of the good, compliant child who acquiesced to whatever came their way?

Some parents, however, refuse to take no for an answer, choosing instead to try their best in overpowering their rebellious kids. Sometimes it works; in many cases, it does not.

It was called the "Devil's Half Acre," a place in Richmond, Virginia, that held the largest slave-trading site outside of New Orleans. Hundreds of thousands of slaves came here. Some of these were the stubborn, defiant ones, sent to be broken by their masters. They were the slaves who kept running away or refused to comply with the directives they were given by their owners. When a master was at his wits' end and didn't want to lose money by killing his slaves, he sent them here to be broken into obedience. When they arrived, they were submitted to unspeakable acts of torture. Some of the men were raped in the hopes of emasculating them into submission.

And it's here where many slaves met Mary Lumpkin (1832–1905).

Mary was a slave and concubine of Robert Lumpkin, the owner of the Devil's Half Acre. When she was thirteen, Robert impregnated her and demanded she serve at this slave-breaking site. Years later, on his deathbed, Robert set Mary and their five children free. Not long after his death, Mary was shocked to discover he had willed to her the Devil's Half Acre.

What would Mary do with this parcel of land which had caused such devastating trauma? Would she not want to ruffle feathers—just settling down to a quiet life and enjoying this blessing all to herself? Or would she, in an act of rebellion, redeem the evil by repurposing it for good?

I think you have a hunch of what Mary did. Instead of using her inheritance for herself, she promptly turned it into an education center for blacks called the Richmond Theological School for Freedmen. Today we know it as Virginia Union University, one of the first HBCUs in our nation. This was Mary's way of getting back at Robert and the many acts of cruelty she had witnessed over the years. Virginia Union stands as a testimony to Mary's defiance of the system that sought to break the spirit of her people.

What was once a place which confined and tortured the body now educates and frees the mind. "Virginia Union . . . was born in the bosom of Lumpkin's jail. The place we were sold into slavery becomes the place we are released into intellectual freedom," says Virginia Union board chair, W. Franklyn Richardson.[1] Or, as many have quipped, "'The Devil's Half Acre' has become God's half acre."[2]

The black church has always held an affection for the Jewish patriarch Jacob, drawn in by his defiance. His very entrance into the world was marked by a fight with his twin brother Esau while in his mother's womb (Genesis 25:22). I don't know how bad the struggle was, but it was so bad Rebekah cried out to the Lord about the turmoil she felt. And once he and Esau got here, they continued to be at odds with each other for most of their lives. When his future father-in-law promised him the girl of his dreams, only to trick him on his wedding day by giving Jacob her sister, he didn't pout and leave; he dug in and worked another seven years for Rachel. At every turn we see Jacob's defiance. It seems as if there is not one person he doesn't have a conflict with, even God.

And in one of the most jaw-dropping scenes in Scripture, the narrator of Genesis says that Jacob wrestles *with God* (Genesis 32:22-32).

I don't even know what to do with this! The best I can come up with is to think of the way I would wrestle with my sons when they were toddlers, allowing them to jump on me and pretending they had pinned me to the ground or beaten me up. But nothing in the scene suggests this was a game or an act. This wasn't the kind of wrestling we see on television which is obviously fake. Jacob and God are going at it. This is next-level craziness. The world has never seen rebellion like this.

Finally, God dislocates Jacob's hip and demands that Jacob let him go.

Again, I just don't know what to do with that.

It's at this point that you'd think the match is done. Carry my boy off the field, into the locker room and order the X-rays. But it's not over. Like a child holding onto his father's leg, refusing to let go as he's dragged from room to room, Jacob latches on and will not call it quits.

I'm at a real loss now, seriously.

Jacob says he won't quit until God blesses him. So God changes his name from Jacob to Israel, because he has wrestled with God and . . . prevailed?

Jacob would go on to father twelve sons whose descendants together would form the nation of Israel, God's chosen people. This nation would be the people of promise, all from a defiant man who had no give-up in him.

One of the descendants of Jacob, okay, *the* descendant of Jacob—Jesus Christ—challenged us to have our own wrestling match with God, and to not be so quick to take "no" for an answer. He told the story of a woman who kept coming to a judge demanding justice, only to be denied time after time after time. But this rebellious woman refused to accept his directive. Just as God did with Jacob, the judge gave in to her persistence. This, Jesus says, is how God wants us to come to him in prayer (Luke 18:1-8).

There are some things God will only give us when we wrestle with him—some blessings we will not lay hold of until after we have struggled with God over a long period of time. What have you stopped praying about because you've yet to see the answer you were hoping for? Who told you to stop praying for what seems to be impossible? Who told you to give up? Of course, we often need to walk in simple obedience, but there's a good kind of rebellion. It's a rebellion that says, "God, I'm just not going to stop until you bless me."

LEAVING PARIS

For consider your calling, brothers: not many of you were wise according to worldly standards, not many were powerful, not many were of noble birth. But God chose what is foolish in the world to shame the wise; God chose what is weak in the world to shame the strong; God chose what is low and despised in the world, even things that are not, to bring to nothing things that are, so that no human being might boast in the presence of God.

1 Corinthians 1:26-29

Some things in life won't get settled until they are faced. The credit card bill is not going away because we don't look at it. Our marriages won't get better because we ignore the problem. And the freedoms of blacks were not secured solely by singing and clapping in church. Inevitably, after the last note was played, they had to exit the premises and face the likes of Birmingham's Bull Conner and his cadre of ornery officers and German Shepherds, anxious to quell any struggle for equality. As the protagonist in Amor Towles's novella *Eve in Hollywood* says, "I want to hear what's happened no matter how ugly, or uncomfortable, or unnerving it might be. Because if we don't stare down the things that make us want to look away, then the world is just a mirage."[1]

James Baldwin (1924–1987) understood this, and we all should be thankful for it.

In September of 1957, Dorothy "Dot" Counts became the first African American to integrate Harding High School in Charlotte, North Carolina. As you can imagine, the school did not roll out the welcome mat for her. She was shaken by the jeers, and her frightened image was captured by a photographer to be plastered on newspapers across the world.

At the same time, the emerging writer James Baldwin was at peace in a local Paris café. No, he wasn't there on vacation. He had made Paris his home, a long way from Harlem, New York, the place of his upbringing. America had become too much for Baldwin. The racism and injustice ate away at his soul. He had found himself in an incessant rage; he longed for not just tranquility, but an environment where there would be no limits on his full embodied self. I can see James Baldwin on a break from writing, seated at the local café, sipping his latte, the tide of rage having gone out to the sea of forgetfulness, scanning the newspaper this late summer day in 1957. And then he sees Dorothy's frightened countenance, and on a dime everything changes. Sometime later, Baldwin would reflect:

> Facing us on every newspaper kiosk on that wide, tree shaded boulevard, were photographs of fifteen-year-old Dorothy Counts being reviled and spat upon by the mob as she was making her way to school in Charlotte, North Carolina. There were unutterable pride, tension, and anguish in that girl's face. . . . It made me furious, it filled me with both hatred and pity, and it made me ashamed. Some one of us should have been there with her! I dawdled in Europe for nearly yet another year, held by my private life and my attempts to finish a novel, but it was on that bright afternoon that I knew I was leaving France. I could, simply, no longer sit around in Paris discussing the Algerian and the black American problem. Everybody else was paying their dues, and it was time I went home and paid mine.[2]

I imagine James didn't stay at the café long that day. The rage had returned, where he took and unleashed it on paper, helping to mobilize the struggle for equality. If Martin Luther King Jr. was the voice of the civil rights movement, James Baldwin became its pen. In 1963, a few years after his courageous return, Baldwin would give us his classic book *The Fire Next Time*, inspiring generations out of their own Paris cafés of complacency and on to the frontlines to fight for justice.

More books would follow, accompanied by a torrent of speeches, interviews, and a famous debate over race relations held at Oxford with white conservative William F. Buckley. Baldwin's pen and presence were bearing down on the global conscience, causing fissures in the status quo of racial inequality.

All this because he chose to leave the comforts of Paris and join in the fight.

The juxtaposition between Baldwin's words and his person is stark. *Rage* is an appropriate word to describe his posture. No, not the out-of-control rage of a forest fire which destroys everything in its path, but more the controlled rage of a fireplace that changes the temperature of the home. To read or hear Baldwin is to be warmed, oftentimes uncomfortably, by his zeal for justice.

And yet to see images and video of him throws you. He's not what you would think. The power doesn't seem to fit the package. Baldwin was a diminutive man whose speech was slightly accented with British tones. And there was a genteel way about him. I mean no disrespect, but if you were in elementary school with Baldwin and were looking for someone's lunch money to take, it would be his. But it is this odd pairing of passion with frailty that made him a giant. To look at Baldwin left people in awe. They thought, *How in the world could someone like this stand up to the outsized problems of our day?*

One of the themes of the Bible is God's uncanny habit of going with the little person. I'm not talking literally (although sometimes that's true—see David versus Goliath), but the ones who are unimpressive. The ones who a Vegas dealer would stack the odds against. In Genesis, we see God turning women who struggle with infertility into the mothers of many. Israel is outnumbered by the mighty

Egyptians, but God opens up the Red Sea; they march into victory, while their enemy sinks in defeat. Gideon takes down Midian with three hundred men. Mary is chosen to bear the Messiah—that's Mary from the Podunk town of Nazareth, from which everyone doubted anything good could come.

And speaking of Jesus: Isaiah says bluntly that he is not what we would think. The Messiah "had no form or majesty that we should look at him, and no beauty that we should desire him" (Isaiah 53:2). Jesus was born among whispers of his mother's supposed immorality. And by age thirty-three, he was a single, poor, homeless man, considered crazy by many, killed in the most shameful way imaginable—a long death on a cross. His followers were seen as uneducated men, who (excluding Judas) were either exiled or killed for their faith.

This theme reaches its apex with the apostle Paul when he tells the Corinthians that God uses what is weak to accomplish his big purposes in history. God will always put us in front of Red Seas, have us face our own giants, or be outmatched by Midian—so that he alone gets the glory. The only thing required of us is a courageous kind of faith—a leaving-Paris kind of faith—that refuses to back down when the odds are astronomical. Repeatedly, life will require us to leave the cafés of our own comfort, to take steps of faith against obstacles beyond our capacity. It's here, at the crossroads of our smallness and life's bigness, that our legacy is found. There will be moments in your life where what you have is inadequate to meet the task at hand. And that's a good thing.

Ever had life leave you feeling small or weak? Sure, you have. In these moments of smallness, God has us right where he wants us.

The underdog James Baldwin found his legacy when he crossed back over the Atlantic to America. Israel found theirs when pinned against the Red Sea. David found his running out to meet Goliath. So did Jesus on Good Friday. And what about you? What's calling you out of Paris? Maybe it's a choice to face that addiction which seems impossible to conquer. Maybe it's time to take steps of courage as you finally face your Mount Everest of debt. It could be that it's time to own up to the lie you have told to a loved one. Or maybe it's the courage required to release someone of an offense which, honestly, feels too big for that. Had James Baldwin stayed in Paris, at the most, he'd be another good writer. But because he left Paris, he stepped into greatness and bequeathed to us a legacy. Do you want good, or do you want great?

Thank you, James Baldwin, for showing us that comfort is no friend of greatness.

BONHOEFFER'S BLACK JESUS

Long before April 8, 1974, when Hank Aaron (1934–2021) broke Babe Ruth's home run record, when he was just a kid growing up in rural Alabama, he saw an airplane flying overhead and announced to his father that he would one day become a pilot.[1] Hank's dad shook his head and told him there was no chance; colored pilots didn't exist. Sometime later, when he informed his father he wanted to be a ballplayer in the Major Leagues, he was met with the same response: "Ain't no colored players."

A few years later, in the spring of 1948, Jackie Robinson and his Brooklyn Dodgers came to Aaron's hometown to play in an exhibition game. News began to spread that Jackie was at the local drugstore, and Hank took off with his friends to catch a glimpse of his hero. After the drugstore sighting, Aaron's dad took him to the game to see Jackie play. Aaron recalls, "After that day, he never told me ever again that I couldn't be a ballplayer . . . I was allowed to dream after that."[2]

There's something about seeing what *is* that inspires what *could be* in others. This is why black contributions to American and world history are so important, and will always hold an essential place in the annals of time. There's something about seeing people who look like me do what I long to do. There's something about seeing those people, against insurmountable circumstances, refusing to take no for an answer—making a way where there seemed to be none.

We need a defiant Mary Lumpkin to show us evil can be repurposed for good. We need to see in Miles Davis's courage how it is possible to be successful without selling out. And we must always keep Alice Parker in view, because she reminds us that being unknown does not mean being unimportant.

Important as these pictures may be for black people, their influence is not copyrighted by blacks to be solely used for blacks. Black history is within the public domain of world history; it must be shared equitably with all. Present-day attempts to restrain or remove our collective story does not just hurt people of African descent. It does irreparable harm to all of us, no matter our ethnicity.

Some years ago, I was standing outside of Westminster Abbey, the historic church where the kings and queens of England and other luminaries are buried. Eager to get inside, I was shocked to see a statue of Dr. Martin Luther King Jr. positioned just outside the abbey. Near to him was the figure of another historic giant, Dietrich Bonhoeffer (1906–1945).

I had heard of the German pastor in my college and graduate studies, and had found my soul warmed by such writings of his as *The Cost of Discipleship* and *Life Together*. Without question, he deserved his place at Westminster Abbey. But what I could not get away from that particular day was the sadness I felt as I looked around at all of the people with their headsets and guidebooks, being fed a very insufficient narrative. It was the same incomplete narrative I was fed in my undergraduate and graduate studies. I wanted to yell, "Bonhoeffer is here because of black history!"

In the 1930s, at the height of the Harlem Renaissance, a twenty-something Dietrich Bonhoeffer came to Harlem as part of a fellowship at Union Seminary (affiliated with Columbia University). He began looking for churches at once, but the white ones he ventured into did not quite do it. He was looking for something more. One day, Bonhoeffer eased his way into the Abyssinian Baptist Church, a church well over a hundred years old and the backbone of Harlem. When Dietrich crossed the threshold of the church, it was under the leadership of Adam Clayton Powell Sr., a pastor who not only preached the vertical implications of the gospel but emphasized the horizontal dimensions as well. For Pastor Powell, it was not good enough to say you were saved if that salvation did not leak out in ways that combatted racism, helped the poor, and bettered the lives of those around you.

Pastor Powell's message resonated with Bonhoeffer, and he could not get enough. As I stared at his statue at the abbey, I tried to picture his German face among the sea of 1930s Harlem blackness. Eventually, Dietrich joined the church, discovered Negro spirituals (which would become a lifelong passion of his), served in ministry, and followed black leadership.[3] And the preaching gave him language for what would become the passion of his short life: standing up for the marginalized against the oppressor.

A strong case could be made that Bonhoeffer would not have gone back to Germany to fight for the oppressed Jews, or participated in the assassination attempt of Hitler which cost him his life, if he hadn't first heard the gospel in all of its glorious implications at the Abyssinian Baptist Church.

Black history made Dietrich Bonhoeffer. No Abyssinian, no abbey.

It was Dr. King, who stands close to Bonhoeffer at the abbey, who said, "We are caught in an inescapable network of mutuality, tied in a single garment of destiny."[4] And while King wrote these words as a rebuke to Birmingham clergy pleading for him to be passive, his larger point cannot be missed: regardless of ethnicity or economic status, we are a connected people. To sever sections of my story does not only harm me; it does harm to all of us.

At a time when the American family is in crisis, we need to learn from our Hispanic siblings and the emphasis they place on *familia*. The steeled determination of the Asian experience and their refusal to act as victims, paired with their communal value of honor, serves us well too. And there is something to be gleaned from our white Western siblings, whose strong emphasis on the individual is a vital piece of the portrait of "mutuality."

Chances are, we will not be graced with a statue outside of Westminster Abbey. But legacy has never been about statues and renown.

Instead, leaving a legacy is about laying hold to all God has portioned us to receive and packaging it for the good of others. And when, on the sojourn of life's road, we face our own mountains and Red Seas, may we lean into the overcoming grace of God.

ACKNOWLEDGMENTS

Grace to Overcome marks my tenth book, and I don't mean to sound trite at all in offering thanks to my Lord and Savior, Jesus Christ. Never in my wildest dreams could I envision a several-decades writing career, and I am more than filled with gratitude.

While it goes without saying that I could not do any of this without the support of my wife and family, along with the generous partnership of my agent Andrew Wolgemuth and the great people at InterVarsity Press for the opportunity and constructive feedback as I wrote this book, I do want to pause and issue an extended thanks to my pastor, Bishop Kenneth Ulmer.

When I first landed in Inglewood, California, to work at Bishop Ulmer's church, the Faithful Central Bible Church, I was more than naive when it came to black history. My three years at the church (while working on a graduate degree at a local seminary) left me in awe, not only at the gospel of Jesus Christ, but at the black presence in the Bible. Neither my Bible college nor seminary ever made mention of Moses marrying a black woman, or Jesus' family fleeing to what my pastor intentionally labeled as "Africa" when their lives were in danger. It was Bishop Ulmer who highlighted the African roots of historic Christianity, as when, according to church history, the Ethiopian eunuch of Acts 8 took the gospel back to his home country. Bishop, I cannot thank you enough for modeling a faithfulness to the gospel of Jesus Christ and the text of Scripture, and for being an unashamed, embodied black man who felt a responsibility to affirm our presence in the redemptive plan of God.

NOTES

INTRODUCTION: CUL-DE-SACS

[1]Isabelle Khoo, "Morgan Freeman Calls Black History Month 'Ridiculous' In Throwback Video," HuffPost, February 10, 2017, www.huffpost.com/archive/ca/entry/morgan-freeman-calls-black-history-month-ridiculous-in-throwba_n_14642958.

[2]Jim Salter, "Missouri School Board that Previously Rescinded Anti-Racism Resolution Drops Black History Classes," *AP News,* December 22, 2023, https://apnews.com/article/black-history-classes-dropped-missouri-school-district-774d11889a15f7418dc47239caec6337.

[3]Anemona Hartocollis and Eliza Fawcett, "The College Board Strips Down Its A.P. Curriculum for African American Studies," *New York Times,* February 1, 2023, www.nytimes.com/2023/02/01/us/college-board-advanced-placement-african-american-studies.html.

[4]David W. Blight, *Frederick Douglass: Prophet of Freedom* (New York: Simon & Schuster, 2020), xvii.

[5]Ryan P. Burge, "Black Americans See the Biggest Shift Away from Faith," *Christianity Today,* February 15, 2022, www.christianitytoday.com/news/2022/february/black-american-nones-faith-unaffiliation-nothing.html.

1. JESSE NEEDS A HUG

[1]It turns out that this letter is an urban legend; there is no evidence of Long writing or sending such a text. To see an Internet post that quotes these

words without citing evidence, see Claire Barrett, "Tell Him How Things Can Be Between Men on This Earth," *HistoryNet,* June 24, 2020, www.historynet.com/tell-him-how-things-can-be-between-men-on-this-earth-jesse-owens-unlikely-friendship.

[2]Malcolm Gladwell, "Hitler's Olympics, Part 7: Long Jump, Tall Tale," *Revisionist History* podcast, accessed October 25, 2024, www.pushkin.fm/podcasts/revisionist-history/hitlers-olympics-part-7-long-jump-tall-tale.

3. THANK GOD FOR A PRAYING MAMA

[1]Monica Holland, "Title IX Pioneers," *The Tennessean,* June 23, 2022, www.tennessean.com/story/sports/2022/06/23/wilma-rudolph-black-american-woman-inspiration-title-ix-pioneer/7666836001/.

5. OLAUDAH "OXYMORON" EQUIANO

[1]Olaudah Equiano, *The Interesting Narrative of the Life of Olaudah Equiano* (London, 1789), in the digital collection *Eighteenth Century Collections Online,* University of Michigan Library, https://quod.lib.umich.edu/e/ecco/004837188.0001.001/110:8.

[2]Equiano, *The Interesting Narrative*, 87.

6. THE DOZENS

[1]Frances Grandy Taylor, "Snapping Back: When Playing 'The Dozens,' Nothing's Off Limits—Not Even Your Mother: All You Need Is a Quick Wit, a Sharp Tongue and a Cool Head," *Los Angeles Times*, May 30, 1994, https://www.latimes.com/archives/la-xpm-1994-05-30-ls-63970-story.html.

7. THE FATHER OF MODERN GAMING

[1]Lauren Smith and Emma Bowman, "Their Dad Transformed Video Games in the 1970s—And Passed On His Pioneering Spirit," *NPR*, September 17, 2021, www.npr.org/2021/09/17/1037911107/jerry-lawson-video-game-fairchild-channel-f-black-engineer.

8. BILLIE HOLIDAY AND HER "STRANGE FRUIT"

[1]Rachel Chang, "How the Government Targeted 'Strange Fruit' Singer Billie Holiday with Drug Arrests," Biography, February 26, 2021, www.biography.com/musicians/billie-holiday-narcotics-us-government.

[2]Martin Luther King Jr., "Remaining Awake Through a Great Revolution," speech given at the National Cathedral, March 31, 1968, quote accessed via www.nps.gov/mlkm/learn/quotations.htm.

9. NOT TODAY

[1]"St. Petersburg, Florida, Orders Public Pool Closed After Black Man Swims in It," Equal Justice Initiative, eji.org, accessed October 25, 2024, https://calendar.eji.org/racial-injustice/jun/8.

11. ZIPPORAH'S HOT COMB

[1]David W. Blight, *Frederick Douglass: Prophet of Freedom* (New York: Simon & Schuster, 2020), 653.

12. BLACK EXCELLENCE

[1]Justin Gamble, "The Cast of 'A Different World' Launch HBCU Tour to Fund Scholarships and Boost Enrollment," March 2, 2024, www.cnn.com/2024/03/02/us/a-different-world-hbcu-tour-2024-reaj/index.html.

[2]David L. Eastman, *Early North African Christianity* (Grand Rapids, MI: Baker Academic, 2021), 20.

13. A MOMENT OF SILENCE FOR ANARCHA, LUCY, AND BETSEY

[1]Camila Domonoske, "'Father Of Gynecology,' Who Experimented On Slaves, No Longer On Pedestal In NYC," *NPR*, April 17, 2018, www.npr.org/sections/thetwo-way/2018/04/17/603163394/-father-of-gynecology-who-experimented-on-slaves-no-longer-on-pedestal-in-nyc.

14. EDWARD'S CROSSOVER

[1]Edward Victor Hill, *A Savior Worth Having* (Chicago: Moody Publishing, 2002), 33-34.

15. COOKIES AND CAGED BIRDS

[1]Maya Angelou, *I Know Why the Caged Bird Sings* (New York: Random House, 2002).

17. THE BLACK BABE RUTH?

[1]Andrew Simon, "Josh Gibson: A Larger-Than-Life Legend," mlb.com, accessed October 25, 2024, www.mlb.com/history/negro-leagues/players/josh-gibson.

20. DON'T WASTE YOUR PAIN

[1]Bruce Marshall, *The World, The Flesh, and Father Smith* (Boston: Houghton Mifflin, 1945).

21. OBAMA'S CROWN

[1]Jackie Calmes, "The Boy Who Touched Obama's Head Is Graduating, with the Ex-President's Congratulations," *Los Angeles Times*, May 27, 2022, www.latimes.com/opinion/story/2022-05-27/barack-obama-photograph-boy-hair-pete-souza-oval-office-graduation.

22. 90 SECONDS TO CAMELOT

[1]Taylor Branch, *Parting the Waters: America in the King Years 1956-1964* (New York: Simon & Schuster, 1989), 362-75.

23. A WARM PRESENCE

[1]Audrey Henderson, "What We Know About Alice Parker, a 'Hidden Figure' in Modern Heating," Energy News Network, February 28, 2022, https://energynews.us/2022/02/28/what-we-know-about-alice-parker-a-hidden-figure-in-modern-heating/.

[2]Alice H. Parker, "Heating Furnace," accessed October 25, 2024, https://patentimages.storage.googleapis.com/60/2a/3d/3177ea24e445aa/US1325905.pdf.

24. I GOTTA BE ME

[1]You can hear Sammy's speech and performance at "Sammy Davis Jr. I Gotta Be Me 1973," January 20, 2011, YouTube video, www.youtube.com/watch?v=1h9REK3HYWQ.

27. EMMIT'S "SHOES"

[1]Anand Subramanian, "Emmit McHenry—The Man Responsible for the .com Phenomenon," *Fun Times Magazine*, March 1, 2022, https://funtimesmagazine.com/emmit-mchenry-the-man-responsible-for-the-com-phenomenon/.

28. WHAT'S MY NAME?

[1]Jared Brock, "The Story of Josiah Henson, the Real Inspiration for 'Uncle Tom's Cabin,'" *Smithsonian Magazine*, May 16, 2018, www.smithsonianmag.com/history/story-josiah-henson-real-inspiration-uncle-toms-cabin-180969094/.

29. WHITNEY'S WAY

[1]*Whitney*, directed by Kevin MacDonald (Los Angeles: Roadside Attractions and Miramax, 2018).

30. THE DEFIANT MARY LUMPKIN

[1]Kristen Green, "The Enslaved Woman Who Liberated a Slave Jail and Transformed It Into an HBCU," *Smithsonian Magazine*, April 4, 2022, www.smithsonianmag.com/history/the-enslaved-woman-who-liberated-a-slave-jail-and-transformed-it-into-an-hbcu-180979757/.

[2]Michelle Miller, "'The Devil's Half Acre': How One Enslaved Woman Left Her Mark on Education," CBS News, October 29, 2022, www

.cbsnews.com/news/the-devils-half-acre-mary-lumpkin-enslaved-woman-left-her-mark-on-education/.

31. LEAVING PARIS

[1]Amor Towles, *Table for Two* (New York: Viking, 2024), 440.

[2]Eddie S. Glaude Jr., *Begin Again: James Baldwin's America and Its Urgent Lessons for Our Own* (New York: Crown, 2020), 31.

AFTERWORD

[1]The title of this chapter comes from Reggie L. Williams's book *Bonhoeffer's Black Jesus: Harlem Renaissance Theology and an Ethic of Resistance* (Waco, TX: Baylor University Press, 2021).

[2]Ed Henry, *Faith: The Rest of the Jackie Robinson Story* (Nashville: Thomas Nelson, 2017), 3.

[3]Williams, *Bonhoeffer's Black Jesus*.

[4]Martin Luther King Jr., "Letter from Birmingham Jail," April 1963, published in *The Atlantic* as "The Negro Is Your Brother," accessible at www.theatlantic.com/magazine/archive/2018/02/letter-from-a-birmingham-jail/552461/.

ALSO BY THE AUTHOR

The Offensive Church
978-1-5140-0597-2

Enduring Friendship
978-1-5140-0844-7